THIS IS OUR WORLD

THE AGE OF KINGS

First published in this edition 1976
Published by William Collins Sons and Company Limited, Glasgow and London

© 1976 illustrations L'Esperto S.p.a. Milan and Tradexim S.A. Geneva

© 1976 English language text William Collins Sons and Company Limited

Printed in Great Britain
ISBN 0 00 106122 4

THE AGE OF KINGS

by Ann Currah

Foreword by James Burke

Collins
Glasgow and London

Contents

Foreword

We live, today, in a world of unparalleled complexity. The flow of information that ought to make that complexity comprehensible has reached the proportions of an uncontrollable torrent. National libraries are unable to say how much is being written, or by whom. The computer has so far been unable to produce a means of providing the general public with access to the information. And yet, access to it becomes more vital, as knowledge becomes more and more specialized.

As the log jam builds up, the development of telecommunications, particularly in the form of television, presents the young people of today with glimpses of a world that their parents already find difficult to cope with. There is increasing concern among the older generation about the need for the kind of information that will enable them to understand and if necessary argue with the changes brought about daily by new developments. It is not that the new knowledge has been deliberately withheld—rather that comprehension demands an ever-increasing expertise in the basic elements of a bewildering number of disciplines.

Again and again in my work I receive letters from parents, and even teachers, asking where they can find the facts that will permit them to explain to their children and pupils why change occurs, and what effects change will have. To such letters, the only possible answer is "read". And yet, where do you go to read, when so many of the thousands of fragmented groups of scientists and thinkers find it so difficult to explain to each other what it is they are doing? There is urgent need, at the adult level, for some kind of common source of data, provided in some common language. Researchers are at present working on such a new language—it's called a meta-language—to answer the problem of translating from English to English.

The dilemma has occurred with the dramatic increase in the sheer number of "things known" over the last half-century. Someone recently said about today's world: "if you understand something it must be obsolete". That is the nub of the problem. The world moves too fast, in too many directions, for anyone to really know more than a tiny fraction of everything there is to know, in any depth. The task, for the adult, is possibly hopeless.

All the more reason that the present-day system of education, which must inevitably equip a child for a career by encouraging specialization, should provide tomorrow's specialist with as wide a grounding in knowledge as possible. It is only with such a broad preparation that tomorrow's specialist will stand a chance of communicating to his fellow members of society. That is why I commend this particular work. It covers an enormously wide variety of subjects, from the nervous system to Alexander the Great and beyond the earth to the stars. Above all, the text is written in such a way as to benefit maximally from use of the way a *child* sees the world. The illustrations are admirably clear, and facts are presented in analogies that a child would use. The work is, I think, a successful attempt to provide easily absorbed, and more important, easily memorable explanations of the world around us. It provides a valuable base on which a young mind can build.

James Burke

Introduction

This book and the companion volumes present a bold, clear
picture of the knowledge man has gained about himself, his earth,
and the universe he lives in. The text is aimed particularly at
young readers of about nine years and upwards. In this volume
four very important centuries in man's social and historical
development are explored—the fifteenth to the eighteenth
centuries. This was a period when life changed greatly for the
majority of men. The power of kings and of the Church was
changing, the structure of society was changing, ideas and
knowledge in all fields were expanding rapidly. New discoveries,
inventions, and ideas excited the imagination of all Europeans.
So did the discovery of the New World. These centuries were the
period when the modern world, as we know it, was beginning.

Young readers' knowledge of these events in man's history is
naturally limited. Helping children to draw on and to learn new
information using their own memories and experience is of great
importance for their understanding of man's progress. As we all
realize, the simple accumulation of dates, names, places, and
events can no longer be a major aim in helping children to learn.
Children today need to be able to adapt to changing knowledge,
to be able to re-learn and to re-think throughout adult life. This
informal encyclopedia sets out to help children to learn to think
for themselves. The means employed are simple.

The pictures are large, colourful, specially planned photographs
and related drawings. The idea behind them is to draw on
children's own knowledge to explain ideas, and to begin to put
historical concepts into simple perspective.

Kings and change

Kingly shadows

In the kingdoms of Mesopotamia and the empires of Persia, Greece, and Rome, kings were powerful men. All the people from the poor farmers to the rich nobles felt the shadow of their king fall over the land. When the states of Europe began to form, the power of kings and the way they ruled changed.

Soldiers and machines

New ways of fighting battles helped change the lives of kings. The Hundred Years' War between England and France lasted until about 1453. Until then battles were called the "sport of kings". Great knights and kings challenged each other to personal combat. The peasant-farmer called into battle by the noble lord who owned his land fought hand to hand with enemy peasants. They roamed the country, setting fire to houses, and stealing anything of value they could find.

At the end of the Hundred Years' War, the Royal Army of France was formed. Then soldiers and machines were used together. Trained soldiers wore uniforms, and obeyed orders together. This, too, was the age of artillery fighting–with cannons and heavy guns. Now kings could raise armies that could roll over unprepared enemies like a steam roller over the road surface.

Kings and money

The Black Death, the plague which raged through Europe in the year 1348, caused as many changes in life as did the Hundred Years' War. The plague killed between one third and one half of the whole population of Europe. As a result, great knights and powerful landlords no longer had enough peasant-farmers (called serfs) to till their lands and to fight their wars. So they began to have to pay men to farm the lands and to fight.

When kings wanted to go to war they could no longer depend on their knights being able to raise armies. Kings, however, could raise money by taxing their people—making them pay a certain sum of money into the royal treasury. But that was not enough to pay for cannons or large numbers of soldiers. So kings had to borrow money to pay large armies. Kings borrowed from their own people. They borrowed money just as today we can borrow from banks.

As more and more peasants moved to the towns, the towns became richer and more prosperous. Peasants became craftsmen and workers in towns and were paid wages. They spent money on food and drink and goods in towns. Merchants who sold goods became richer. Some of these rich merchants became bankers—they could lend money not only to craftsmen and other traders, but to landlords, to princes, and to kings.

One king's dream

King Charles V, Holy Roman Emperor, was born in the Netherlands in the year 1500. This was more or less in the middle of the change from ancient days to modern. Before 1500, we think of man's history as being very ancient—there were knights in armour, Charlemagne's great Holy Roman Empire in Europe, and before that the empires of Rome and Greece, and before that even the rise of the ancient civilizations round the Mediterranean Sea. After 1500, the states or nations of Europe began to live a way of life that was more modern.

Charles V had a great dream—he wanted to rule again a united and even expanding empire. Charles inherited from his family the rule of many lands. First of all, he was king of Spain. He was also named Holy Roman Emperor. He ruled the lands of Burgundy in France, much of Germany, and the American and Italian lands conquered and discovered by Spain.

His great dream of unity and peace ran into much trouble in his lifetime. The times and ways of life were changing too swiftly for one king to rule a huge European empire under the authority of the Church. Charles's Spanish subjects hated him and rebelled. His German subjects began trying to limit the power of the pope and the Church. His brother, Ferdinand, who was king of Bohemia and Hungary, took over his German lands.

Meanwhile, further discoveries of lands in the New World across the Atlantic Ocean made people in the kingdoms excited and restless. There were many wars and great frictions between the peoples in Europe. In 1558, Charles gave up his dream and became a monk. His lands passed on to his many relations.

15

Language problems

Charles V tried to unite, or bring together, many different people in his Holy Roman Empire. This was difficult, and the king had problems. The people in his huge empire thought differently about all the important events of the day—wars, religious ideas, trade, and so on. They lived different everyday lives.

One special problem was that they had different languages. Charles spoke French. The people he ruled spoke Spanish, German, French, Dutch, and Flemish. This was a serious problem, because Charles could not talk directly to his people or to his soldiers. He needed an interpreter, someone who could translate what someone said to him into French.

Today the problem of people speaking different languages is not so serious. At the United Nations in New York, or at the European Common Market headquarters in Brussels, there are skilled men and women who can translate or interpret words from one language into another quickly. These translations can be broadcast over microphones to people in their own language. They can then understand what other people are talking about. During Charles's reign, this did not happen.

The Arc de Triomphe in the centre of Paris, the French capital city, was built during the reign of Napoleon. It is a magnificent symbol of France and of the French people's pride in their nation.

A poor king or a sorry emperor

Charles V had inherited part of France for his empire. The French, however, were proud. They refused to become part of the Holy Roman Empire. The French king was Francis I. His personality was almost opposite to that of Charles. Francis loved costly and beautiful things. Beside the rivers of France he and his court built beautiful castle-like homes, called *châteaux*. These were famous for their splendour and beauty. Francis taxed the French people heavily to fill his royal treasury and to pay for his extravagances.

When the young Charles declared war on Francis, he joked: "Soon he will be a poor king or I shall be a sorry emperor." Through most of Charles's reign, he and Francis were rivals for power. They were at war from about 1517 until 1559. In this time they signed five peace treaties, but none lasted. In fact, the wars went on until the French were exhausted and short of money. In the end, neither side had gained nor lost a thing. Perhaps Charles was not sorry because he lost no territory to the French. But the war was useless. Because of it, Charles did not spend enough time keeping Christian Europe and the Church united. So the European states grew ever more independent, and the Church ran into great difficulties.

Out of pocket

The kings in the sixteenth century (the years 1500–1599) had a serious problem which concerned the Holy Roman Church. For many years, kings and priests had depended upon each other for their power over ordinary people. During this time, kings began to try to gain some of the Church's power for themselves. But ordinary people were growing angry with the Church. It seemed that the Church grew ever richer, while they grew poorer and more out of pocket

paying to both kings and Church.

Peasants, farmers, craftsmen, and traders had to pay heavy taxes to their kings. The Church demanded much money too. People had to pay for religious ceremonies, and even to be forgiven for their sins. Many men began to ask why the Church did not pay taxes, and why the Church owned so much land, when ordinary men did not. They asked why churchmen should be so rich, while other men were so poor. Men began to realize that churchmen were more anxious to gain wealth and power than to perform humble acts of worship.

21

The fires of Church reform

Clipping the Church's power

In the sixteenth century, changes in the Holy Roman (or Catholic) Church affected the whole history of western Europe thereafter. These changes are called the Reformation. The men who inspired them intended to reform the Church. Reformation means a "change for the better". The men who started the Reformation wanted to improve and better their Church.

Their ideas about what the Church should do and should not do were shocking at the time. But as often happens with new ideas, they passed quickly from town to town, and from country to country. The Reformation spread like wildfire from Germany, to England, to the Swiss and the French, to the Scots, and to the Dutch. Once the fires of reform had been lit, the Catholic Church seemed to be aflame with arguments about the rights and wrongs of religious ideas. From this time onwards the Church and the Holy Roman Empire would never again have the same power over men and their lives. The Reformation kindled a new kind of religious light in men's hearts. It trimmed the Church's power just as clippers could trim the spires of a cathedral cut out of cardboard.

Heaven or Hell?

From the time of knights in armour (the Middle Ages), people thought that making money was the work of the devil. The Church taught that making too much money would ensure that a man went to hell. Men who were faithful to God, and who had only enough money for their own needs, would go to heaven. There were many fables about rich merchants. These fables told of men who lent money to others being carried off to hell or finding that the money in their boxes had turned to dried leaves.

As more and more men flocked to towns, buying and selling

became important in daily life. Townspeople did not like the Church overseeing trade and business. They had to exchange money to live. So they found unpleasant the Church's ideas that trade may be necessary but was harmful to the soul. It became obvious that the churches were getting richer than the traders and merchants. Also the Church often took money given to it by traders and money-lenders to build new churches. Sometimes both the Church and the kings borrowed money from merchants and tradespeople to pay for armies to go to war. Whether money-making was the work of the angels or the devil became a burning question at the time of the Church Reformation.

Bill posting

The Reformation began in a little town in Germany with a simple act of bill-posting. Martin Luther, a church monk and university lecturer, nailed to a church door in Wittenberg a piece of paper called the *Ninety-Five Theses*.

These theses were ninety-five arguments against the Church's selling of indulgences. Indulgences were pardons for sins sold by priests and monks for sums of money. Luther was specially angry about the sale of pardons in Germany by a man named Tetzel. Tetzel toured Germany in 1517 selling pardons. He hoped to raise huge sums of money to rebuild the beautiful church of St Peter's in Rome, the capital of the Holy Roman Church, and the pope's home.

Martin Luther became a monk when a very good friend of his was struck by lightning and died. Luther felt he owed his own life to God's mercy. For a long time Luther was unhappy as a man of the Church. He felt he was too sinful to be a good monk. Slowly he realized that a sinful man like himself could gain peace if he truly believed and trusted in his own faith in God. Luther felt that the Church's selling of pardons for the sinful ways of men did not lead them to trust God. So Luther was particularly upset by the selling of indulgences. He was furious when some of his own students and others at Wittenberg sneaked away to buy pardons from Tetzel.

Cleaning up

Martin Luther had meant to clean up
a practice of the Church's that he
thought was evil—the selling of
pardons. In his *Ninety-Five Theses*, he
wrote that he would argue his ideas
on the rights and wrongs of selling
pardons. But the Church was not
going to argue with him. The practice
of selling pardons brought in too
much money. The Church would not
let people even discuss Luther's ideas
in public. The Church ordered Luther
to withdraw his theses. He refused. So
he was excommunicated, or expelled,
from the Church.

Unfortunately for the Church,
expelling Luther did not stop talk
about his ideas. From all over
Germany, men spoke up in support of
him. From Luther's first simple ideas
came more powerful ones on how to
reform the Church and give it a
thorough cleaning. The Reformation
had begun.

Rally of support

Luther had dared to question the authority of the Church. He had dared to rebel against Rome. Every class of people in Germany felt that Martin Luther had dared to do what they had wanted to do. He had said in public what they had felt for so long.

Thousands of men rallied to Luther's support. Peasant-farmers who had suffered awful hardships under their landlords felt that any kind of change must help them. The landlords and knights, who were afraid that the growing towns and rich traders would make them poorer, supported Luther. Great princes and wealthy merchants, who had their eyes on the Church's lands and monies, joined Luther. Tetzel was mobbed by people and forced to stop selling his pardons. In some towns, monks, priests, and bishops were afraid to wear their church robes for fear of being attacked by angry people. When Luther was expelled from the Church, all his supporters were aflame with anger.

An offer of a lift

Martin Luther began to ask whether or not the Church in Rome should rule people's everyday lives. People all over Germany began to hear about Luther's ideas. Many believed that a new age of freedom was coming. Many people agreed that the Church had too much power and too much wealth.

Charles V grew worried. He called Martin Luther to a meeting in 1520 to defend his ideas. The priests and rulers of the Church thought that Luther was spreading dangerous thoughts. So at the meeting they announced that it was now a crime for anyone to give Luther shelter or to support his ideas about Church reform and freedom.

This did not worry many powerful northern German princes. They liked Luther's ideas. They wanted more power for themselves. They wanted the Roman Church to be less powerful. So they supported Luther and they gave him shelter in their castles. It was as if they offered a poor, simple monk and church scholar a ride in their expensive cars. The tired monk who was used to walking was grateful for the offer of a lift. He accepted their support. These northern princes set up a new, Protestant church, the Lutheran church. This new church was based upon Martin Luther's ideas. It became very powerful in the north of Germany.

If the shoe fits...

"If the shoe fits, put it on," is an old
and wise saying. It means that if a
new idea or a new way of life or
anything else suits someone, he or she
should go ahead and accept it.

The Reformation of the Church
suited thousands of people. It gave
them hope of more personal freedom
from the Church and from the State or
the kings. The beginning of the
Protestant Reformation gave people
the freedom to think for themselves,
rather than to obey unthinkingly the
order of their superiors. Martin
Luther began this Protestant
Reformation.

Many other scholars and churchmen took up his ideas and added to them. John Calvin, a Frenchman who preached in Geneva, Switzerland, said that man should have religious freedom (as Luther had said), and also political and social freedom. Calvin said man's only duties were to God. John Knox took Calvin's ideas to Scotland. England became divided between the old and new faiths. From this time on the Holy Roman Church was no longer the only guardian of faith in God. Men from all walks of life could now have a personal, independent relationship with God.

The business of faith

The ideas which had sprung from the teachings of John Calvin were an important form of the Protestant faith. Lutheranism had been popular with peasants and then with princes. Calvinism was popular with the middle classes—with traders, merchants, and bankers. These men, engaged in trade and industry, were changing the way of life of people in Europe from a backward, rural, farming life to a prosperous town and city life.

Calvin taught in Geneva, a city teeming with business life. No longer a city of peasants and princes, Geneva was a place of respectable, free businessmen. The men who were drawn to Calvin's ideas saw that the qualities needed to be successful in business were the same as those needed to be a good Christian: thrift, hard work, soberness, and modesty. Suddenly, it seemed that men no longer need fear that being successful in business would endanger their chances of reaching heaven. They could dedicate their private and their business lives to the glory and service of God. Businessmen were welcome in God's church, and they became steadfast in their worship.

The Renaissance

Rescue of old cultures

The word Renaissance means rebirth. The word is used to describe an exciting period of time when the art and literature of ancient Greece and Rome were rediscovered. The Renaissance is also a period of great advances in learning in all fields and a period of discovery.

This rebirth or Renaissance began in Italy in the middle of the fourteenth century. In the years between 1340 and 1540, the Italian cities produced a rebirth of culture that had not been seen in the world since the glorious days of the Greek statesman Pericles, and mighty Athens.

It is easy to understand why the Renaissance began in Italy. Italy is a land where the marvellous marble ruins of the Roman empire still glow in cities, towns, and the countryside. The Italians inherited a tradition of learning from classical (ancient Greek and Roman) times which never quite died out. Then too the Italian cities were rich. The Italians were expert traders and merchants. The princes of the Church and the State were rich and could pay artists, craftsmen, and scholars for their work.

The Renaissance flourished for almost two hundred years in Italy. This furious burst of creative activity passed on to other European countries in the sixteenth and seventeenth centuries. The beautiful written prose of France, the magnificent poetry and theatrical drama of England, the music of Germany followed the burst of art, architecture, and learning in Venice and Florence. They were the foremost Italian Renaissance cities.

The rediscovery of classical learning was very precious to the western world. For the men of Italy took the ideas and thoughts of the masters of Greece and Rome out of moth balls. During the Middle Ages, the work of great Greek philosophers and thinkers like Socrates, Aristotle, and Plato had almost been forgotten. The paintings, pottery, sculptures, and buildings of Greece and Rome had almost been forgotten. The ideas about science and mathematics, politics, and how men could achieve a satisfactory way of life had almost been forgotten. The Italians rescued this culture. It was as if they opened their own cupboard and wardrobe doors and discovered exciting things which had been preserved in mothballs from ancient times.

Men and immortality

The men who began studying the ancient learning of Greece and Rome were called the New Humanists. They were interested, as the ancient Greeks had been, in man, the human being. Before the Renaissance, in the Middle Ages, scholars had taught that man was of little importance. Man was only a soul to be saved. The hard ways of life and the loss of faith in the Church changed this idea. Renaissance men again began to believe that man's mind and his achievements were exciting. The New Humanists began not only to re-acquire the old learning, but also to look at nature and the world with questioning eyes.

The renewed interest in man and the new spirit of questioning spread beyond the learning of Greece and Rome. Curiosity about all areas of life was displayed by Renaissance men. They tried to be like the ancient Athenians, educated in many branches of learning and accomplished in many arts and crafts. They were proud of their learning and talents. They loved glorious works of art. They adored personal glory. They worshipped the immortal works of classical art. They desired immortality for themselves. Painters and sculptors strove to provide their wealthy patrons with immortality or everlasting fame. These portraits show how handsomely the Renaissance artists succeeded in achieving immortality for their patrons.

Truth before beauty

A Dutchman, Erasmus of Rotterdam, was a great scholar who lived during both the Renaissance and the Reformation. Erasmus believed in truth before beauty. He urged men to study the Bible to learn true faith. The baby Jesus, Erasmus reminded men, had been a naked human being, not a fancily dressed baby princeling.

Erasmus was not only a loyal Christian Catholic, he was also a Humanist. He studied and translated Greek and Roman works of learning besides the Bible. He even edited the famous *Geography*, written by Ptolemy the ancient Greek scientist who lived in Alexandria, Egypt.

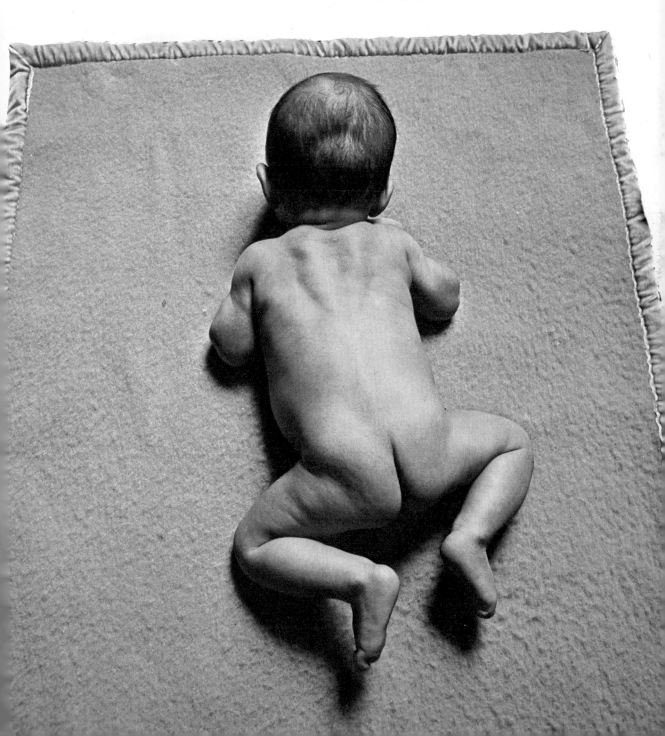

Studying oneself

The idea that man was interesting and important was exciting to men and women of the Renaissance. The idea that much could be learned by studying how men's bodies and minds worked seemed new and fascinating. The Renaissance was a rebirth of man's own interest in all the many activities of man. The Renaissance might have taken for its motto the famous saying: "The proper study of mankind is man himself."

The new study of man showed in many ways. People realized that education was important. Children could develop all their abilities if they were given a chance to learn as many things as possible. Men and women of Renaissance times are famous today for all the things they could do well. Some men were artists, writers, scientists, scholars, and musicians all rolled up in one.

The paintings and sculpture of men and women took on a new lifelike look. Artists were no longer happy with flat, lifeless imitations of people. The Emperor Charles V recognized this when he saw portraits by the famous Italian painter Titian. Charles refused to let anyone else paint him. Titian's portraits were so lifelike the people in them seemed to breathe.

In the sixteenth and seventeenth centuries, the study of mankind was reflected not only in education and art, but in music, in politics, and in written works. Europeans were caught up with the new interest in man. A Frenchman, Michel Montaigne, followed the Renaissance ideas and became one of the first modern writers. In 1580 he wrote personal essays about himself and the nature of man. One of his most famous works, *On Friendship*, is a discussion of friends which is funny, wise, and truthful. Montaigne wrote as if he had studied his mind and body with a magnifying glass. So do many writers today.

Springtime spirit

The coming of spring after a cold dark winter is a joyous time. So too, the coming of the Renaissance after the bleak Middle Ages was a time of joy, gaiety, and beauty. Springtime and the Renaissance have much in common.

The magnificent painters of Renaissance Italy show us in their pictures how colourful life was and what pleasure people took in beauty. Opposite is part of a picture of young people painted by Sandro Botticelli. It is called *Spring*. Botticelli came from Florence, one of the great city-republics of Italy, and the home of many fine painters and artists. Under her ruler, Lorenzo de Medici (called Lorenzo the Magnificent), Florence became one of the two greatest Renaissance cities. Her famous artist sons included Michelangelo. He painted the Sistine Chapel in Rome, the private chapel where the pope prays. Michelangelo also carved the *Pietà*, a most beautiful statue of Mary and the baby Jesus.

Venice was the second great Italian Renaissance city. Art and beauty challenged the glories of ancient Athens in this handsome city built on lovely winding waterways. Venice and Florence were not the only cities where the love of beautiful things was reborn and grew. All over Italy, the spirit of spring in artistic and in everyday life burst into flower, took root, and spread throughout Europe.

The Renaissance man

To call someone today a "Renaissance man" means that he or she is well-rounded or gifted in several kinds of activity. This phrase is used because the most famous men of the Renaissance excelled in many activities.

Above all others, three Italians stand out from other men as being almost perfect examples of Renaissance men. These men are Leonardo da Vinci, Michelangelo, and Leone Alberti. It is difficult to choose, but perhaps Leonardo is the greatest.

To begin with, Leonardo painted two of the most famous and valuable pictures in the world. One is the *Last Supper*, which shows Jesus and His twelve disciples. The other is the *Mona Lisa*, shown on the opposite page, which hangs in the Louvre Museum in Paris today. It is sometimes surprising to think that the painting is not finished. Leonardo was a busy man. Perhaps he never had time to complete the portrait. He is famous as a painter and also as an architect and engineer. He designed drains and waterworks for the city of Milan. He invented fortifications and war machines. He studied music. He studied the bone structure of humans and animals.

Michelangelo is famous for his statues and for his paintings. He portrayed the human body beautifully, and used it to show his deep religious spirit and love of nature. Michelangelo, too, was skilled in building fortifications. During a long siege he managed to save the city of Florence due to his engineering skill. When he was over seventy years old, he composed some of the most beautiful sonnets (a kind of love poem) ever written in the Italian language.

Alberti is not as famous today as he deserves to be. He is an outstanding example of a well-rounded Renaissance man. He was a Humanist scholar and a great architect who wrote ten books on building. He was the finest horseman and athlete of his day. He wrote delightful songs, wrote one comic play, painted pictures, and even invented a machine for raising ships sunk in the sea.

Science – old and new

The rebirth of man's interest in the old Greek and Roman learning changed everyday life. As they studied ancient scholars and looked at the world with renewed curiosity, men began to question how and why things were as they were. Educated men no longer only praised God for the miracle of the sun shining. They tried to find out why the sun shone. Men did not just look at creatures in nature with humble wonder. They tried to find out how birds really flew, or how living animals breathed and moved. While men had used simple machines for centuries (like the wheel or the lever), they began to try to make better machines to do more of man's everday work.

With the Renaissance, or rebirth of learning, came the scientific renaissance. The rebirth of interest in the old sciences led to a new interest in practical science. This was very important in man's history. The scientific renaissance became, in time, a scientific revolution. Knowledge in all the different kinds of science improved and changed. Together with all the other changes in men's lives, the scientific revolution laid the foundations for today's world and for tomorrow's future.

The men who practised the new science did not have the kind of equipment to work with that today's scientists have. Equipment and tools had to be invented as science studies progressed. They experimented with simple things as school children do today. We can imagine that men's early science experiments were similar to school projects. For example, a class might build a small plastic rocket, with a windmill device to lift it up, and an electric battery for power. In the early days of science, there were no plastics or electric batteries to work with. These things, and many others, would have to be invented in the coming years.

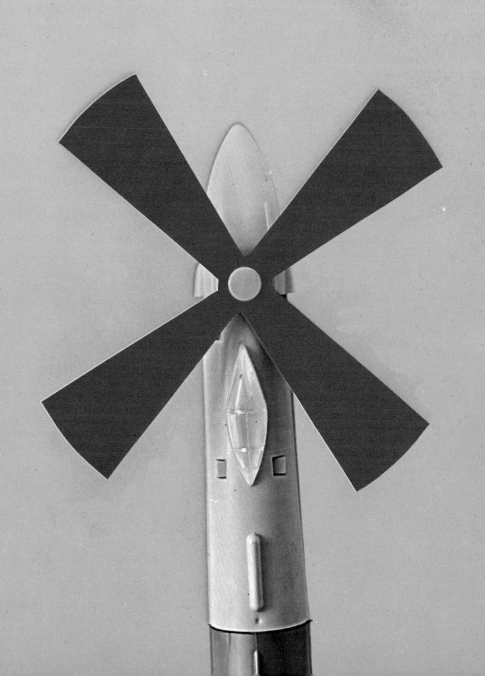

Science takes wing

The renaissance in art and learning, the Protestant Reformation, and the scientific revolution all changed men's lives. The revolution in science took wing because the Reformation and the Renaissance led men to think more freely about the nature of life.

The scientific revolution began when the Humanists rediscovered the knowledge of ancient Greece and Rome. Aristotle, the ancient Greek philosopher and natural scientist, was one of the first rediscoveries. He had tried to describe and group the different kinds of insects, animals, and plants that could be seen on earth.

Leonardo da Vinci, the great painter, was also a student of science. He studied the human body and its bone and muscle structure. Leonardo studied insect and animal bodies too. He was a keen observer of nature. Leonardo studied the wing structure of insects and birds. This led him to write about the flight of birds and to try to design a flying machine. The picture shows what Leonardo must have observed: butterflies have a double set of wings. Butterfly wings are surprisingly similar to the first planes man managed to fly in our own century—the tiny bi-planes.

In the Renaissance, men began to think in a new way about the structure and the laws of nature. These first thoughts would lead them to today's scientific ideas and inventions.

Art and life

The Renaissance artists showed the beauty of life. They also showed man and nature in a very real manner. One of Michelangelo's famous statues is of David, the king of Israel who as a boy slew the giant Goliath with a stone. Michelangelo's *David* showed the beauty of the human body, but the artist added something more. He showed the intelligence of a man, and his real-life bones and muscles. These details do not detract from the statue's beauty. They add grandeur and a sense of wonder.

The ability of Renaissance artists to increase the dignity of man and life by showing both beauty and realism spread to the other forms of art in Europe. Beethoven and Bach were great German composers who could capture and hold the joy and the tragedy of life and nature in deeply moving music.

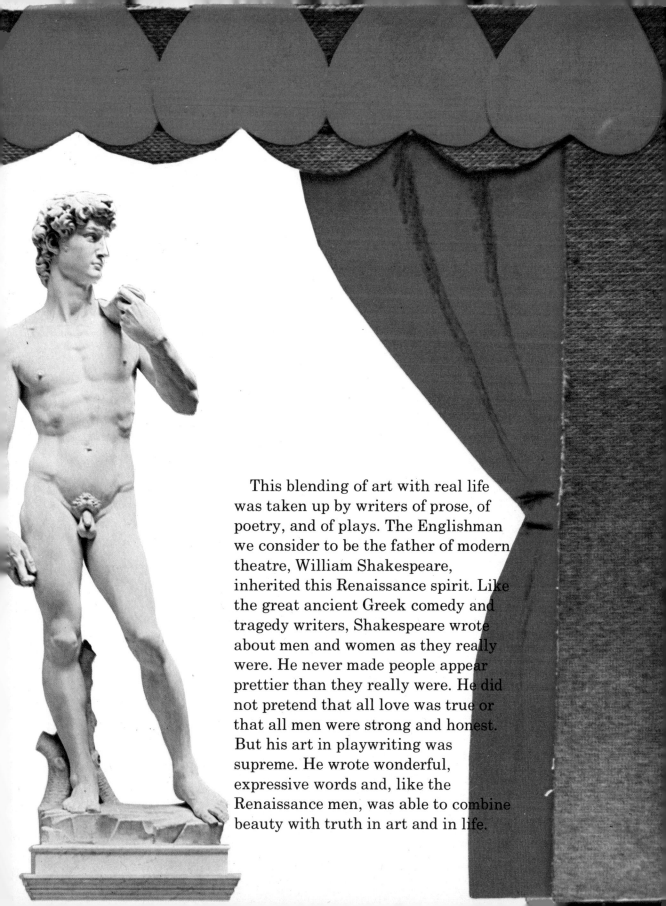

This blending of art with real life was taken up by writers of prose, of poetry, and of plays. The Englishman we consider to be the father of modern theatre, William Shakespeare, inherited this Renaissance spirit. Like the great ancient Greek comedy and tragedy writers, Shakespeare wrote about men and women as they really were. He never made people appear prettier than they really were. He did not pretend that all love was true or that all men were strong and honest. But his art in playwriting was supreme. He wrote wonderful, expressive words and, like the Renaissance men, was able to combine beauty with truth in art and in life.

The end justifies the means

A very famous man of the Renaissance was Niccolo Machiavelli. Machiavelli was a writer and statesman from the city of Florence. In a short book called *The Prince*, he wrote the words: "The end justifies the means." In this book he wrote about how princes and rulers governed men's lives. *The Prince* was one of the first books on political science. Political science is the study of how men are, or how they should be, ruled or governed.

The ancient Greeks and Romans wrote about how men could be governed more wisely and happily. Machiavelli studied their works, but he saw that men were often not ruled wisely. Rulers were often cruel and evil, but still powerful. In studying Renaissance politics and ways of ruling, Machiavelli realized that the end often did justify the means. He was not approving of evil methods of ruling, but he said they often worked and were sometimes the only way princes could keep power. This shocked people, then and today. Truth is often shocking.

Machiavelli wrote that princes were often justified in doing evil if they wished to keep their power or to gain a particular goal. The goal, or the end, justified the way, or the means, of achieving it. This was like saying:

"Part of an apple is rotten. I will cut out the rotten part, and staple the apple together. Then I will have a whole clean apple to eat. (Of course, you will have to forget that you might die if you eat the staples.) The end (a nice clean apple) justifies the means (stapling over the cut-out rotten parts)."

Machiavelli's writings were not published until after his death. Then they were banned for many years. Naturally princes and rulers did not like his ideas about how they ruled.

An uneasy mixture

Different as oil and vinegar

Charles V gave up his kingdoms and became a monk. In 1558 he died. The changes in the ways of ruling, in art, in everyday life, and in the Church, all made Charles's attempt to keep the Holy Roman Empire together a failure. The future in Europe belonged to the nation-states. These ambitious states did not join forces or mix together easily. There was friction between kings and queens and between small and large states. They all wanted more power. They all wanted a bigger share of the gold and silver flowing in from the lands newly discovered across the Atlantic Ocean.

The sixteenth and seventeenth centuries were a glorious and romantic period of adventure and rivalry. There were great marriages between rulers. These were not love matches. They were attempts to build bigger, more powerful states by joining them together. There were many wars and land and sea battles. All were attempts to prove one state more powerful than another.

The states of Europe did not and could not work or mix together. They were now too different. They were like oil and vinegar. For a short time a mixture might be formed. States might become friends or allies by marriage, war, or treaty. Then they would separate and go their own ways. Spain, Austria, the German states, France, the tiny Netherlands, and little England were all ambitious for power and wealth. Their rulers were cunning and crafty. They were all determined to see their own country, small or large, grow richer, more powerful, and more and more independent.

Smoothing over the patterns

The king who managed to turn France from a country of small provinces ruled by powerful dukes into a modern nation was Henry IV. When he became king of France and Navarre (a tiny kingdom between France and Spain in the Pyrenees Mountains), the French people were quarrelling among themselves as fiercely as a family trying to decide on patterns for redecorating the walls.

All the great French dukes, their families and supporters, had different ideas about how France should be ruled. There was bitter war between Huguenots (French Protestants) and Catholics. On St Bartholomew's Day in 1572, Catholics murdered hundreds of Huguenots in a really horrible religious blood-letting.

However, Henry managed to unite the dukes and common people and the Catholics and Protestants under his rule. Henry had been born Protestant, but he became a Catholic. This calmed the Catholics down. Then he gave the Huguenots the right to worship safely in a few special towns. Henry also took away many of the dukes' powers.

Henry had faced some very serious problems, but he proved that it was possible to smooth over different patterns of life, even when men of the same nation were bitterly divided in matters of religion and ruling power.

Different appearances

Religious differences from the time of the Church Reformation often made it difficult for European states to become true nations. In the different countries, the people were themselves alike, but outwardly they were Protestant or Catholic. So it was difficult to unite a nation. In 1555, the Germans decided that the religion of their individual states would be decided by the religion of the state's ruler. This was one solution to the problem of which religion to follow.

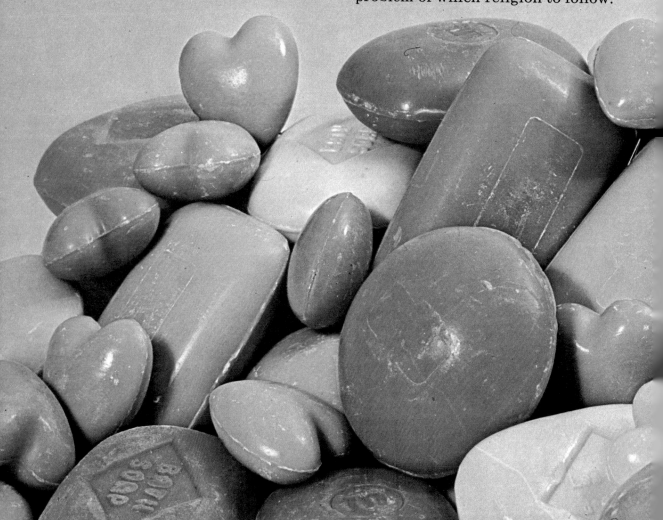

Outwardly the German states appeared as different as these bars of soap. Underneath, they were all made of the same material—they were all Germans. In 1618, this excellent balance of similarity and difference was ruined by the beginning of the Thirty Years' War. It was supposed to be a religious war, but the rulers of Europe turned it into a power struggle. Catholic rulers supported Protestants, and the opposite happened. Germany suffered terribly, her lands laid waste, her princes and common people made poor. It took Germany hundreds of years to recover and become a more modern nation.

The faithful at war

Charles V spent his life fighting the new Protestent faith. He lost the battle, and Europe split among Protestants or Catholics. A Counter-Reformation (a movement *against* the Reformation) began in the Catholic Church, but it was too late.

Once some rulers tasted freedom from the pope, from the Catholic Church, and from the Holy Roman Empire, they determined to stay free by fair means or foul. Bitterness between Protestants and Catholics helped the rulers. When they wanted to grab Church lands or property or when they saw a chance to grab more power, they used religion as a good excuse to go to war.

So the peoples of Europe, faithful to their new Protestant or their old Catholic faith, went to war for God, for king, and for country. All the European countries and their rulers engaged in conflicts in this period carried on in the name of religious faith. Catholic and Protestant rulers from many countries of Europe fought for thirty bitter years on German lands. Catholic Spain attacked Catholic Portugal, and then made war on Protestant England and the Netherlands. Protestant rulers supported Catholic rulers if they thought they could gain something for their own country. High and low, Protestant or Catholic, on the land and at sea, the people of Europe fought each other in the name of God.

Islam packs up in the West

Another threat to the unity of Europe and to the Church existed and should not be forgotten. This was Islam, the religion of the followers of Mohammed, the prophet from Arabia. The Moslems, or followers of Mohammed, had poured out of their vast desert countries and settled in the Bible lands, along the coast of the Mediterranean Sea, in North Africa, and even in Spain. The Christian Crusades tried to destroy the threat of Islam, but they only turned it aside for a while. Then the people of Turkey took up the banner of Islam. They captured Constantinople, the capital of the eastern part of the Holy Roman Empire in 1435.

During his reign Charles V had to fight off attacks by Moslem Turks in the Balkan Mountains on Europe's eastern borders and around the Mediterranean Sea. Turkish pirates attacked ships off the Italian coast.

Thousands of Christian Europeans were made Turkish slaves. They spent their lives miserably, rowing in the swift Turkish pirate ships. In a great sea battle at Lepanto in 1571, one of Charles V's sons defeated the Turks with the help of a huge Spanish and Venetian fleet. From then on, Christians in the West no longer feared a massive unloading of Turkish soldiers and weapons on their shores. Now the Turks had to pack up their soldiers, weapons, and boats. They travelled overland to invade India, where Moslem rulers rose to power.

Up and down

Charles V's son Philip was given Spain, Portugal, the Low Countries, and parts of Italy and the New World to rule. Philip was rather like a powerful earth-moving claw. His personality was cold and hard. He ruled his empire with an iron hand. Philip had many problems during his reign, but he lifted Spain up to the height of her power and greatness.

Philip helped his people to develop the newly discovered American lands which sent gold and silver to enrich Spain. During his reign, the Moslem Turks were defeated at the sea battle of Lepanto. Then, Islam no longer threatened Christian Europe. The Low Countries (Holland, Belgium, and Luxembourg) rebelled against Spanish rule with help from England. Parts of the Low Countries were Protestant and hated Catholic Spain. Philip tried to defend the Catholic faith all over Europe. Spain and England were friendly until Elizabeth became queen. Then relations grew strained. England even defeated the mighty Spanish navy, the Armada, which had set sail to conquer England and win back the English to the Catholic faith.

At the end of Philip's life, Spain was hugely in debt. Europe did not fear Spain since England had "singed the King of Spain's beard", as the Armada defeat was called. Spain slipped from her peak of power when Philip's iron hand no longer ruled.

Pirate power

Pirates have robbed ships ever since man first took to trading by sea. In the seventeenth century, some rulers overlooked the fact that pirates were outlaws. Pirate power was valuable to rulers who wished to challenge mighty Spain. Pirates could move more or less freely in their own countries—as long as they stayed in their own homelands they were safe. Once they put out to sea, they had to rely on their own courage and skill to survive. If caught, they would be hanged for the crime of piracy.

Spain shipped gold and silver in huge quantities from the New World. While the Spanish had become skilled at fighting the Moslem Turkish pirates in the Mediterranean Sea, they never really learned how to fight English and Dutch pirates.

Sir Francis Drake became famous as the terror of the Spanish treasure fleet. In small swift ships like his *Revenge*, Drake could catch and cripple a Spanish ship with cannon fire almost before its crew knew the ship had been attacked. On his many voyages, Drake became the first Englishman to sail round the world (in 1580). Elizabeth, Queen of England, gave him a knighthood and joked about his being a "pirate". Later Drake became a commander of the English fleet which defeated the Spanish Armada. Drake was a hero to all the English nation.

Travel, trade, and change

Obstacle course

Travelling is an important part of men's lives. Travel is enjoyable, but it is also necessary. Today a thousand-kilometre or thousand-mile journey can be taken even by a baby. A car can travel that far in two days. So can a train. Sea voyages take longer. Aeroplanes are the fastest of all. Accidents can happen, and once in a while there are difficulties. A car may have a flat tyre. A train might approach a tree or rocks fallen across the rails. Usually, journeys today are fun and interesting—for business or for holidays and pleasure.

Two or three hundred years ago, a journey was like an obstacle course. In fact, until this (the twentieth) century, travelling has always been as difficult as an obstacle race. The wheel and the sledge were invented by man in very early days. Horses, donkeys, elephants, and other animals were tamed for riding or for drawing vehicles. Men invented boats and then sea-going ships in ancient times. But travelling was awkward, uncomfortable, slow, frightening, and dangerous.

Man must travel, no matter how

difficult or dangerous the journey. He needs to travel to buy and sell food, clothes, and other articles. He needs to travel to find out what other men are thinking and doing. New ideas and new ways of doing things are passed from country to country by travellers. Because journeys were once so hard, news of discoveries and inventions travelled slowly. There are always men who will risk an exciting journey—to make money buying and selling goods, to discover new lands no one else has yet seen, to make war, to settle in a new place and start a new life. So slowly the changes which were occurring in everyday life were passed on by travellers to other men.

Travel, trade, and textiles

Although journeys were difficult, in the sixteenth and seventeenth centuries the roads of Europe were thronged. Many ships sailed the inland seas, the rivers, along the coasts, and even the world's oceans. By risking journeys, men could make much money.

This was the age of merchants. They were men who would risk large sums of money to send men and animals overland to India and the East to buy spices, silks, and other goods which would sell for huge prices in Europe. They would send ships to seek new sea routes to the East, or treasure in new lands.

Beautiful textiles (woven cloth) such as this patterned material from Flanders were in great demand and many merchants first made their fortunes buying and selling textiles in Europe. The skill of weavers using simple hand looms was remarkable. Some of the richest men of the sixteenth century were common people who first made money in the cloth trade. As they grew even richer, they began to trade in other goods. Some merchants whose fathers and grandfathers had been cloth traders became so rich they could lend money to others. These men were the first merchant bankers. Kings, queens, princes, and even the popes borrowed money from merchants.

Doves of peace

Society, or the way of life of individual men in their small communities, slowly began to change in the sixteenth century. For hundreds of years, men and their families had lived in small villages, farming the lands. Many began to escape to the towns where there was more freedom. There they could learn a trade or a craft. They would receive wages for the goods they made or for the work they did. Men could not become rich just by going to live and work in the towns. One way they could acquire money was by becoming traders. Traders could start in a small way. They could sell something they made for more than it cost. With this money they could buy something else, and sell it for a little more. Slowly they could build up a hoard of money.

After a few more exchanges of goods for money, a trader might have enough to lend to someone else. For the loan of his money, he would charge the person who borrowed an additional sum.

Money-lending was a popular way to make money in the towns. Small traders often became big merchants and big money-lenders too. Merchants such as the Lombard Bankers of Italy who could lend large sums were welcomed by princes of the Church and by royalty wherever they travelled. Merchants and money-lenders could travel with no fear in any country. They were like doves of peace.

Costly religious wars were always being fought and rulers needed more and more money to keep their power. So money-lenders and merchants were really the most powerful men of all.

Town men, countrymen...

There were many changes in the life of men in the sixteenth and the seventeenth centuries. Business life grew up in the towns. Different areas of land in western Europe slowly grew into states and nations. The Roman Catholic Church lost much of its power.

New kinds of work were available in the towns. Money could be made by businessmen, traders, and merchants. Life in towns became important, but the land was still most important in people's lives. Real wealth, safety and security lay in owning land rather than in owning goods or in having large amounts of money from trade. The sons of old or noble families who owned large areas of land might go to the towns to learn the trade of merchants. Merchants in turn often bought themselves large holdings of land. The basic things needed for everyday life still came from the land. So merchants often retired to the country to live off the land, abandoning their ships in ports, and leaving their offices and warehouses and businesses in the towns.

Common men become noblemen

From the beginnings of civilization, the society of man has been divided into groups or social classes. These classes were based largely upon the kind of work men did. In the early civilizations of ancient Mesopotamia, Egypt and Persia, people were grouped into different classes. The grouping took the form of a pyramid with a king, or prince, at the top of the pyramid. Then, in the first and most important class, came the priests of religion. In the next class were noble warriors (called knights in the Middle Ages) and soldiers. At the bottom of the pyramid was the large mass of people. These were traders, craftsmen, and farmers or peasants. Sometimes people changed their class. Soldiers could become princes or kings. Common men might become soldiers or even priests. Usually a man was born into a class—the same as his father—and stayed there.

From the 1500s onwards it became possible for more people to change classes. They could improve their position in life by moving upwards into a class that commanded more respect. This happened because of the changes in society at the time.

Almost everywhere in Europe, the "old" noblemen lost some of their power and respect. "New" noblemen began to acquire some of the power and respect for themselves. Many

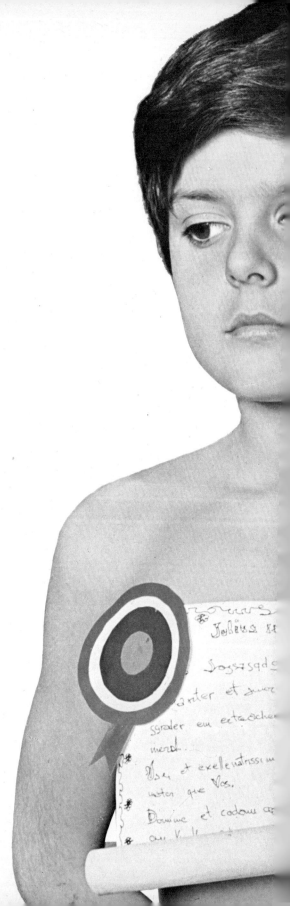

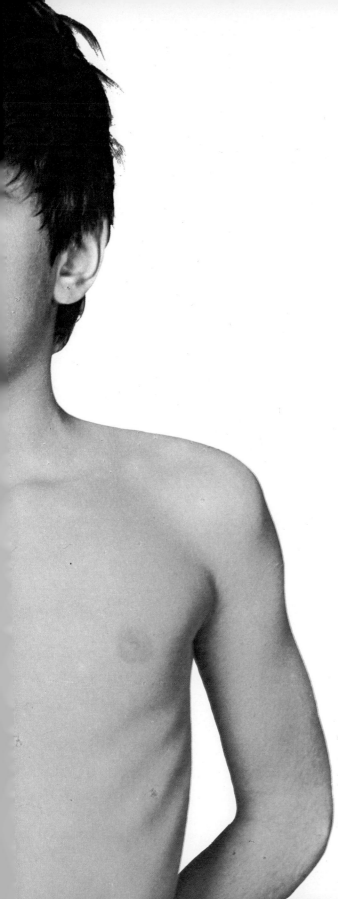

were common men who had made money as traders and merchants.

Kings and queens always rewarded their subjects for loyal service. If a man helped a king to win a war, he might be granted a large estate of land. Or he might be rewarded with a large sum of money. Or he might be given a title—the king might make a common soldier a knight. Then John Common Soldier would be called "Sir" John Common Soldier and his wife would become "Lady" John Common Soldier. This sort of reward was given by many kings and queens in the western European states and countries.

As rich merchants and traders rose to power, they too wanted to become sirs and dukes—they wanted the respect which ordinary people gave to titled, noble people. The merchants and traders found it fairly easy to buy themselves a noble rank. It became common practice in the European countries for monarchs to fill their treasuries by selling titles to newly rich people. Many new knights, barons, dukes, and even earls were newly rich merchants, lawyers, or big bankers. For large sums of money, the monarchs' secretaries would inscribe in elegant handwriting beautiful parchment documents which showed that the rich person held a title and certain areas of land. With these pieces of paper proving their "nobility", the rich former commoners gained the respect they desired.

Land enclosure

Enclosure is the placing of something inside something else. Putting fences or barbed wire or hedges round farming land is an act of enclosure. The enclosure of land in the states and countries of Europe brought great hardship to the many farmers and peasants who lived by tilling the land.

As the numbers of people in the towns grew, they needed more food (which they did not grow themselves). So, many landlords or landowners decided that they could make more money by fencing off areas of land to make them safe for grazing cattle. When these cattle were fattened, they could be sold in the towns for food to make a good profit for their owners.

As the population of towns grew, the trade in woollen goods grew too. People needed to buy clothing. Merchants found a bigger market for both rough and finely woven wool material. So more land was fenced in to provide safe pastures for sheep. The enclosing of pastures for cattle and sheep became more and more widespread in England and other countries.

Thousands of peasants had to give up farming. Some, of course, became shepherds or farmhands. Many left the enclosed lands to try to find work in the towns and cities.

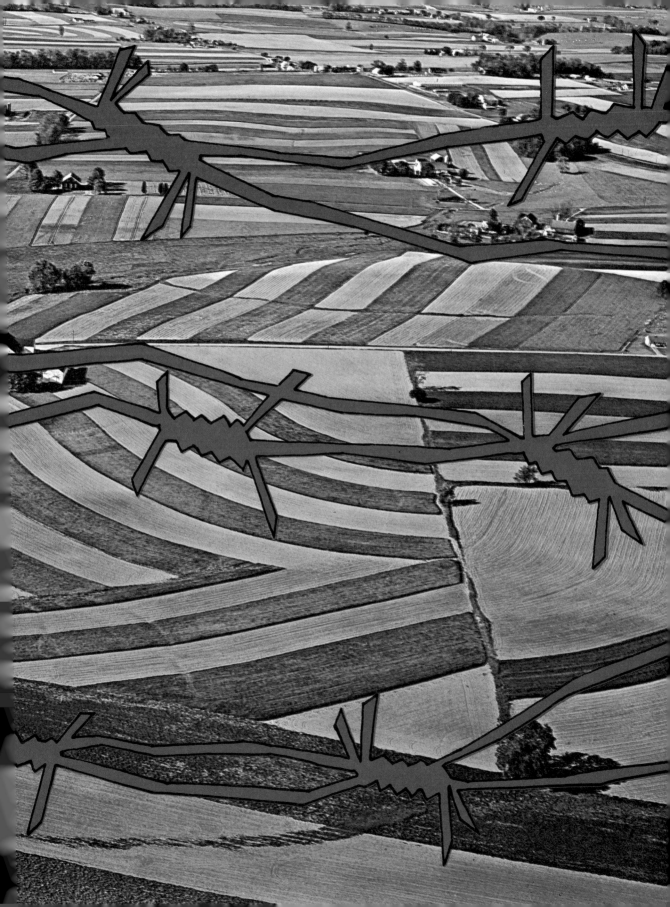

Industry begins

In the sixteenth century, business began to get bigger. The scientific revolution was barely begun, so there were few machines to make goods. The making of clothes, the growing of food, and the building of houses by slow hand labour could not keep up with the growing numbers of people in each country.

The textile merchants were among the first to find new ways of producing more goods. They gave peasants pieces of raw cloth to sew up in their homes and paid them for the finished garments. They organized the first textile factories. This was the beginning of industry, where businessmen employed many labourers in one place to produce large quantities of goods. Sometimes groups of merchants put money together to pay labourers, to provide spinning wheels, looms to weave cloth, and places to sew.

Kings helped merchants because new industry could make their countries rich with more goods to buy and sell. Sometimes kings gave merchants a Royal Charter. A charter gave a group of merchants the right to produce one kind of goods, perhaps woollen cloth. By royal order no one else could make that kind of goods. Charters specially helped England and Holland become rich by encouraging merchants to spend money.

Three new rivals for power

Sailor merchants

From the sixteenth century onwards, Europe was no longer
united. The Holy Roman Empire was no longer the strongest
power in Europe. European people were divided, too, by their
different forms of religion. Smaller countries began to grow more
powerful. They began to have different forms of government and
ways of doing business. The former powerful countries of Europe
became less powerful. Spain grew poorer. Italy was overrun with
foreign rulers. Protestants and Catholics fought religious wars in
Germany. In the north of Europe, three new rivals were rising to
power: Holland, England, and France. Holland and England were
the Protestant powers. France was the Catholic power.

In an age when sea voyaging and trade expanded together, the
Dutch became the most successful sailor-merchants in the world.
Their tiny country was surrounded by ocean and the Dutch were
expert fishermen used to making their living from the sea. An old
Dutch saying is not surprising: One sailor equals three farmers.
For Dutch sailors made their tiny country both rich and powerful
among the European countries.

equals

The people's bride

Elizabeth came to the throne of England at the age of twenty-five
in 1558. Her long reign was a glorious age for England. She is
sometimes called Gloriana, and the age is called the Elizabethan
Age after her. During Elizabeth's rule, England became a sea
power and a trading power. Elizabeth and her wise advisers
encouraged Englishmen to be proud, daring, and successful.
Elizabeth was a skilful diplomat at a time when there was discord
between the European powers. Many rulers and noblemen sought
her hand in marriage. They hoped to control England by
controlling the queen. Elizabeth knew this and declared she was
married to her people. Englishmen adored their proud, wise
queen for they knew she would serve their interests. She told her
last parliament that they had never had a ruler who ever loved
them better. Elizabeth kept England united by treading a careful
path between the beliefs of Catholics and Protestants. Her
relationship with the Spanish, the French, and the Dutch were
careful. Sometimes she favoured one, sometimes another. At her
death in 1603, England was one of the most powerful, independent
countries in Europe. The bride had served her people well.

A few people on the throne

In the 1500s and 1600s, people were divided in their opinions on how countries should be ruled. Some thought that a king should rule absolutely and should not have to answer for his actions to anyone but God. This is called absolute monarchy. Other people thought a country should be ruled by a few able men. This kind of government is called an oligarchy. The word oligarchy comes from two Greek words meaning "a few" and "to rule". The Dutch Republic (Holland) was ruled by an oligarchy. A republic is a country ruled by representatives of the people. The republic's oligarchy was composed of men representing Holland's seven provinces, or states. France was ruled by an absolute monarch.

England had its king and its parliament. Parliament was an assembly of men representing the counties and towns of England. They met to discuss common problems, to make laws, and to raise moncy for wars and other needs. Parliament was jealous of its power in helping to govern. Parliament would not support an absolute monarch. No king could rule without parliament's support. James Stuart, who followed Elizabeth onto the throne, and his son Charles found this to be true. From 1642 until 1648, the English fought a civil, or internal, war. Protestants and parliament's supporters fought Catholics, the king, and the Anglican Church's supporters. Parliament's supporters won and beheaded King Charles in 1649. In the same year, England became another "Protestant republic" like Holland. The representatives of the English people "climbed the throne" to rule their land.

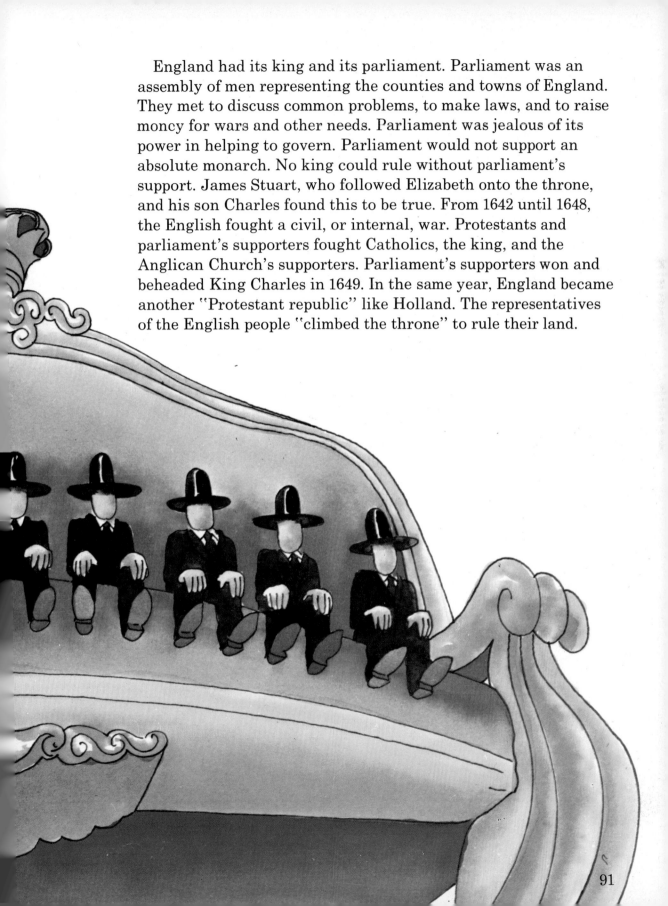

A rose and a tulip at war

Most European countries were ruled by absolute monarchs. The Protestant English and Dutch people challenged royalty's absolute rule. These two great sea powers were traders with much in common. On one side of the English Channel the rose bloomed, a symbol of England's power. On the other side, the Dutch tulip bloomed.

The first fifty years or so of the 1600s are known as Holland's Golden Age. Then the country became a world power. The Dutch East India Trading Company became more successful and richer than the English East India Trading Company. The Dutch became the world's bankers. They made great inventions in map making, in sea navigation, and in science. Painters, poets, and great thinkers bloomed.

In the same century, under Elizabeth, the English age of glory bloomed too. Trade and farming, literature, arts, the sciences and the theatre flourished. England's most famous playwright, William Shakespeare, was alive.

Slowly the English rose and the Dutch tulip became rivals. They drifted into war with each other. They had fought in other parts of the world where their big trading companies were business rivals—in the East and West Indies, and in North America. In 1651 the first shots were fired when England tried to stop Dutch ships transporting so much of the world's goods in their ships. In this short war, both countries displayed amazing feats of seamanship and courage. England finally won in 1653, mostly because she had a bigger fleet. The Dutch asked for peace. The war had proved that the English were the masters of the sea—a role they would play until our own century with an immense effect upon man's history.

A monarch's mannequins

A mannequin is a wooden or plastic dummy which displays
clothes in shops and stores. A dummy mannequin cannot think.
It cannot move by itself. All its movements or poses must be
ruled by a human being. Louis XIV (the fourteenth), King of
France from 1643 until 1715, treated his subjects like shop
mannequins. Louis ruled France alone. No Frenchman did
anything without the knowledge or approval of his king.
Frenchmen existed only to do exactly as he wanted them to do.

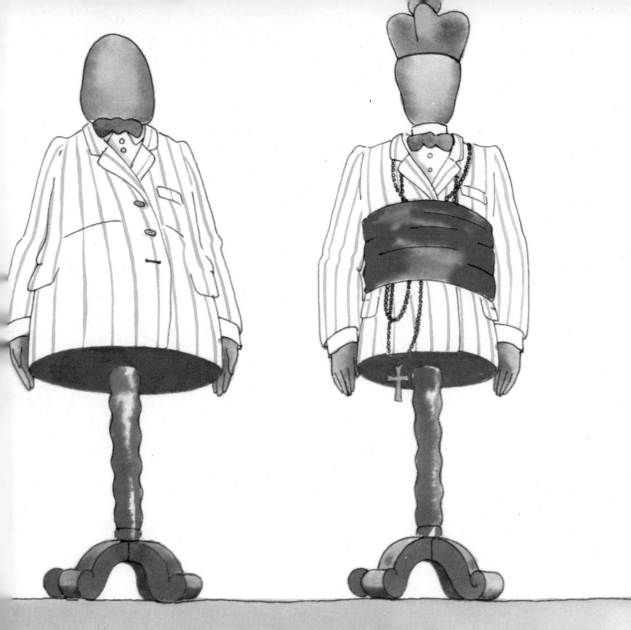

Louis made sure that advisers to his court, soldiers, businessmen and noblemen, and powerful churchmen, had little real power. This was very different from England or Holland, where the monarchs ruled with the help of their people. Louis was an absolute monarch. Under his rule, Catholic France became very powerful. Louis fought a number of wars during his reign. He was jealous of England's trading power. He tried to destroy Holland's business power. He tried to push the borders of France towards the River Rhine in Germany. By the end of his life, all Frenchmen were tired of fighting other Europeans.

$$Q < 2\sqrt{K} \qquad 1+1=2$$

$$\alpha = \frac{P+\sqrt{K}}{Q} > 1 \qquad \frac{1}{2} f\left(\frac{P}{Q}, K\right)$$

$$2\times 2 = 4$$

$$3-1=2 \qquad 6 \qquad x_3 = a_3 + x \qquad 1-1=$$

$$\frac{30}{3}=10 \qquad \left|\beta - \frac{P}{q}\right| < \frac{1}{\sqrt{8q^2}} \qquad \beta = nq$$

$$3 \qquad 9$$

$$x^2 = a + 1 \qquad \lambda_j - \lambda_i > l(x_i, x_i); \qquad 6$$

$$\frac{P_m}{P_\alpha \cdot P_\beta \dots} \qquad 5+5=10 \qquad \frac{2\tan\varphi}{1-\tan^2\varphi} = \sqrt{3} \; \frac{\tan\alpha + t}{1-\tan\alpha \cdot tc}$$

$$a \cdot b + 3 = 8 \qquad y = \frac{a}{2} \qquad 6+1=7$$

A practical man

Louis XIV is supposed to have said: "*L'état, c'est moi.*" In English, this means, "I, myself, am the State." In other words, he alone was the government of France. Louis, however, had some very good advisers. One, particularly, was Jean Baptiste Colbert, the son of a French merchant. Colbert was a very practical man. He understood trade and business, mathematics and how to make money. Although Colbert wore the elegant robes of a minister of Louis, he was a good government official who helped make France strong in money matters.

Colbert, as French finance or money minister, kept careful state accounts, records of money spent, taxes collected, and debts owed. He encouraged French merchants to expand their trade and to seek out new lands across the oceans for trading.

He founded many naval schools and helped develop the French navy. He founded academies, schools in which the arts and sciences were studied. He helped raise money for the many wars of Louis. He tried to make sure that people paid their taxes into the royal treasury.

Colbert was one of the greatest French ministers of government who ever lived. The king's choice was a wise one, and Colbert was loyal and helped make his king's reign glorious.

The Sun King

Louis XIV was called the Sun King. There were many reasons for this name. We know that Louis ruled France as an absolute monarch. He ruled with help from only a very few trusted men like Colbert, his tax collector and finance (money) minister.

During Louis' reign, France became the most admired country of Europe. All other European countries looked to France as a guide in fashions, in manners, in ways of living. At the centre of France stood Louis and his magnificent court at Versailles, outside Paris.

Louis built Versailles, probably one of the most beautiful palaces ever constructed. It was huge and had a fantastic Hall of Mirrors. It was surrounded by wonderful gardens with splashing fountains and exotic plants and flowers. At Versailles lived many, many French noblemen. There they were under the watchful eye of Louis. He could make sure they didn't plot against him.

L'ENTRÉE DE LOU
D'APRÈS CHARLES LE BRUN. ATELIERS

Louis put on wonderful entertainments to keep his court amused. Balls and dances were held, and hunts, sports events, and games like blind man's buff and croquet. Mock battles were staged. Exciting plays and musical shows were put on for everyone's enjoyment. Everything was done to make sure that the ladies and gentlemen did not grow bored or engage in political power plays.

The court at Versailles was so glorious that to the rest of the world it shone and sparkled like the sun. Throughout Europe, people tried to imitate the French court. All of Europe was like a crowd of spectators watching a wonderful play. They followed the goings on at the French court with rapt attention, just as theatre or cinema audiences today watch plays or films.

Artists painted the French court and people could see what it looked like. News and gossip about the court spread all over Europe. The French court circled round Louis like planets orbiting the sun. And in their turn, the states of Europe followed the movements of France. The Sun King was well named.

Upsetting the balance

Man questions the answers

The beginning of modern times in Europe was a period of great change. New ideas about government and how countries should be ruled stirred men's minds. There was great religious conflict. The different classes of people were slowly changing. In science, too, came a time of startling change.

Ever since the ancient Greek scientists, men had believed that nature worked in an orderly fashion, that everything in nature was in harmony or in balance. This depended upon natural laws which could be discovered by reason, or clear thinking.

The ancient Greeks sought to know *why* things worked as they did. If they saw a ball balanced on a flat wooden plank set upon two cactus plants, they would nod wisely and explain why the ball stayed still. It would not have occurred to them to ask, but *how* will the ball behave if only one of the plants grows? They would probably not have tried an experiment to find out.

In the late sixteenth and seventeeth centuries, men began to ask just such questions. They began to try to find out exactly *how* things worked. They stopped just explaining *why* things worked. This questioning upset the balance in scientific thought. Men began to observe nature and scientific things. They began to keep detailed notes, to make experiments, and to ask more and more *how* questions. The answers to their questions were sometimes startling. They changed the whole course of man's life on earth.

Blind man's buff

Science before the sixteenth century was conducted rather like a game of blind man's buff. The scientists themselves more or less played the role of the blind man. Their guesses and ideas about how things worked in nature now seem to us the work of men who were blinded to the true nature of things.

Some of the old ideas about science amuse us today. For hundreds of years people really believed that the earth was flat and that the sun revolved round the earth.

As we know, during the fifteenth century, and the period of time known as the Renaissance, or rebirth, men rediscovered all the things the ancient Greeks and Romans had known. Once men had studied again the old knowledge, they began to learn new things and to ask new questions. This was the beginning of a new age of science.

One of the important things to remember is that the new scientists did not just decide that all the things the Greeks and Romans had learned were wrong. They realized some of the knowledge was very important. The new scientists worked with the old ideas about the nature of things. They changed and added to them. They made some corrections. Above all, they believed as the ancient Greeks had, that there were no limits to what man could learn.

A light in the dark

If you were bored with all your toys
and games, you might decide to start
looking for something new to play
with which would give you a new idea
for a game. Perhaps you might decide
to search in the attic among the old
clothes, furniture, and toys. You
would not discover much that was old
or new if you had no light. You might
rummage about in the dark for a long
time without discovering anything
to excite your imagination.

If you shone a light into the attic,
you might suddenly come upon a most
beautiful old treasure. You might
discover an old-fashioned china doll.
She would give you ideas for new
games to play.

Strange as it may seem, many new
scientific discoveries were something
like rummaging round in an attic.
Scientists would think and think
about the old ideas. Then, suddenly,
a new thought would come to them.
The new thought would be like a light
shining in the dark. The new thought
would lead them to new ideas and
these would lead them to startling
new discoveries.

Mathematics – and the first modern scientist

Mathematics has been called the language of science. Maths help scientists to discover new things and to explain how things work. A child will be asked to add two and two together. When he learns that the answer is four, he is beginning to understand mathematical relations. Maths is the science of numbers and their relationships to each other.

   Below is a picture of the ground and some everyday objects on it. The picture is all about mathematical relationships too. It has been drawn by a computer. The computer is the most advanced mathematical machine modern scientists have invented. It helps scientists today to discover new things more quickly.

The first great modern scientist was also a mathematician.
He used his knowledge of maths as modern scientists do today—
to help him make new discoveries and explain how things worked.
This scientist was Galileo Galilei. He lived from about 1460 until
1524, and he taught at the universities of Pisa, Padua, and
Florence in Italy. Galileo wrote exciting books about his ideas
and discoveries. Galileo proved that the earth and planets whirl
round the sun, by using mathematics and the telescope. Because
of this, he was the first great astronomer, or star scientist. Galileo
discovered that a pendulum, or weight on the end of a string or
rope, could be swung back and forth and used to measure time.
He saw that solid objects fell at the same speed regardless of their
weight. Mathematics helped him in all his work.

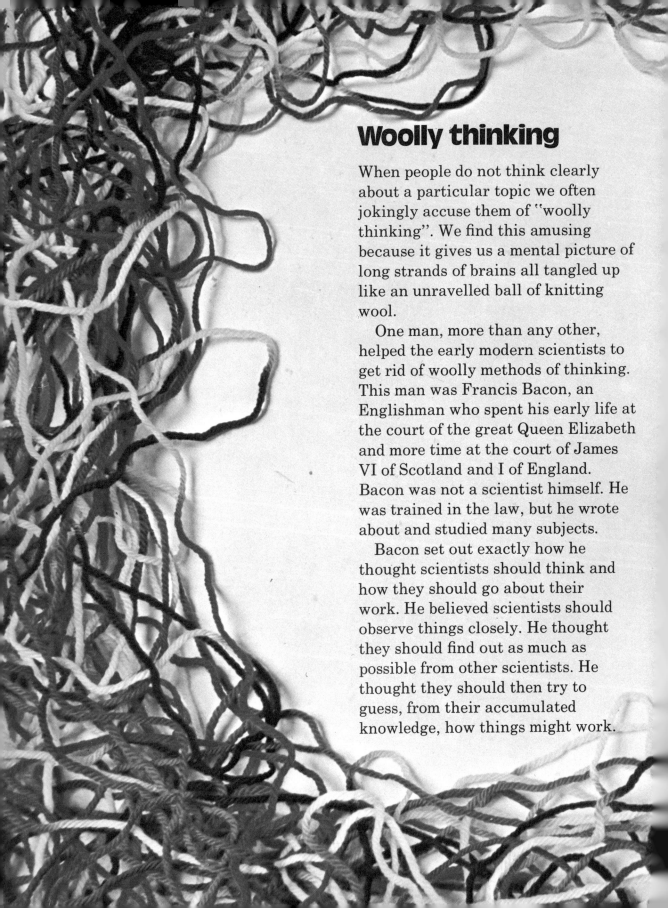

Woolly thinking

When people do not think clearly about a particular topic we often jokingly accuse them of "woolly thinking". We find this amusing because it gives us a mental picture of long strands of brains all tangled up like an unravelled ball of knitting wool.

One man, more than any other, helped the early modern scientists to get rid of woolly methods of thinking. This man was Francis Bacon, an Englishman who spent his early life at the court of the great Queen Elizabeth and more time at the court of James VI of Scotland and I of England. Bacon was not a scientist himself. He was trained in the law, but he wrote about and studied many subjects.

Bacon set out exactly how he thought scientists should think and how they should go about their work. He believed scientists should observe things closely. He thought they should find out as much as possible from other scientists. He thought they should then try to guess, from their accumulated knowledge, how things might work.

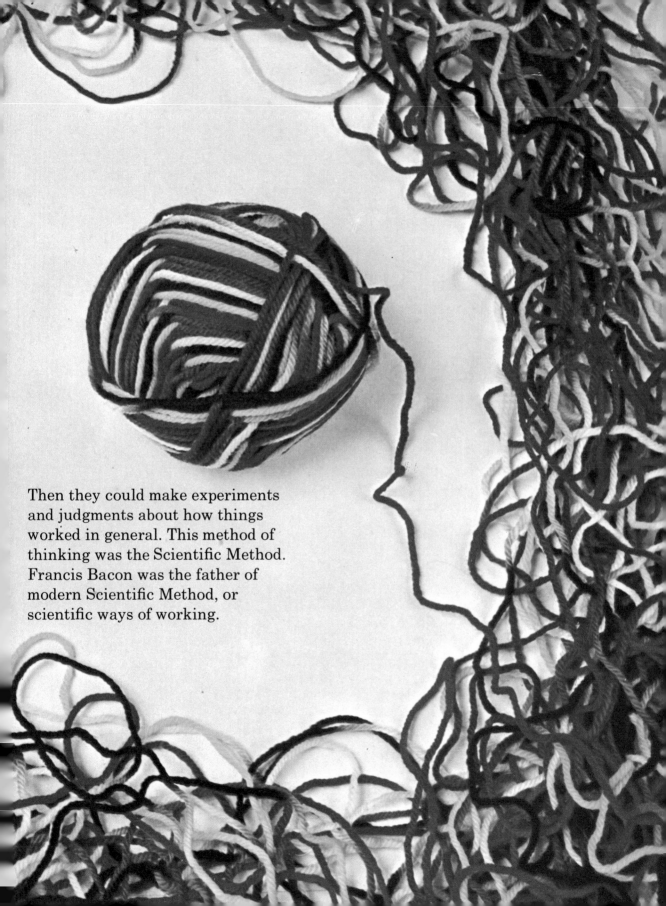

Then they could make experiments
and judgments about how things
worked in general. This method of
thinking was the Scientific Method.
Francis Bacon was the father of
modern Scientific Method, or
scientific ways of working.

The heavenly bodies

For hundreds of years, people had many strange ideas about the earth and the planets, which they called heavenly bodies. Sometimes people even imagined that the planets had faces. The idea of the "man in the moon" is very old indeed. Since the days of the ancient Greeks, most people believed that the earth stood still while the sun, moon, and planets and stars moved round it. An early scientist from Poland did not believe this to be true.

Copernicus, who lived from 1473–1543, began to think that the earth and planets moved round the sun. He wrote a book called *The Movements of the Heavenly Bodies*. He also explained that the earth spun round in space like a top, and that the stars were very far away from the earth. Later Galileo proved with his telescope that Copernicus' ideas were true. These ideas about the place and movement of heavenly bodies were exciting to men. Because Copernicus was the first to write publicly about these ideas, he is known as the father of modern astronomy.

Scientists and craftsmen

Before the new age of science, scientists had been scholars. They spent their time studying the ancient books, and talking with other men of learning. Craftsmen did practical work. They built cathedrals or made tools and simple machines. Now scientists needed the practical skills of craftsmen. Craftsmen began to help with scientific work. As ideas changed about the earth, the planets and the stars, scientists needed better telescopes, pendulums, and instruments for measuring time.

New practical tools had to be invented to help make better discoveries and to help gain more knowledge.

The working together of craftsmen and scientists was very important in the history of science. Together, practical inventions and scholarly study made modern science and modern scientific progress possible.

Harmony
before discord

Signing the peace

Louis XIV of France created many conflicts in
Europe in the seventeenth century. The English
and the Dutch fought with each other, and against
France. The European powers feared that Louis
would claim the Spanish throne and that France
and Spain would try to rule Europe. At last,
England, Holland and Austria, defeated France.

In 1713, the European states signed official
papers which proclaimed a great peace. Europe
was at rest at last. The bitterness between peoples
of different religions and of different nations
slowly died down. People seemed more in tune
with each other. It was as if the pegs of a violin
were being turned. With each turn, the strings
were stretched until at last the instrument could
be played in tune. A new harmony and a new spirit
of good will was felt by men. The Age of Reason
was beginning, a new age of harmony based on
natural laws rather than on bitter divisions.

The good housewife

In 1740 a young woman became Empress of Austria. She was Marie Theresa. The new empress, or queen, found the empire of Austria in a shambles. The royal treasury was empty. Other European states wanted to rule Austria and its lands, and were prepared to fight to get them. The Austrian army was defeated and depressed.

Like a good and careful housewife, Marie Theresa set about cleaning up the mess and restoring order.

In this century, the Austrian empire was the remains of Charles V's great Holy Roman Empire. Marie, a descendant of Charles, inherited the rule of many lands. She was Empress of Austria, Queen of Bohemia and of Hungary; she ruled over Silesia, parts of Germany and Belgium.

Under her rule, a high court of justice was set up. The army was reformed and became a better fighting force. Life for peasants tilling the lands was made more secure by regular payments for their work and the right to rent the land they worked. By 1774 a law said children between six and thirteen must attend school. High schools and colleges were set up to educate the common people better. There was even a private academy named the Theresianum, after the empress, to educate sons of noblemen. Marie Theresa's good sense made life better for the whole Austrian empire.

The military machine

One of the states most feared by Austria and other European states was Prussia. Prussia began as a small state called Brandenburg, in the centre of Germany. Slowly Brandenburg's lands expanded. This powerful state, whose capital was Berlin, became known as Prussia when it took over the small state of Prussia from the kingdom of Poland.

A Prussian general once said that his country was "not a country with an army, but *an army with a country* that served as its headquarters and food supplier". From the time of the Emperor Frederick William I (1713–1740), other countries looked on Prussia as a dangerous military machine. The emperor's father and grandfather had believed in strong armies, and they had built up the power of Brandenburg-Prussia. Frederick William was a "drillmaster-king", a harsh, near madman who called his army the "basis of his earthly bliss". Under his rule, the Prussian army became the fourth largest in Europe (about 83,000 men). His country was only tenth in size.

In Prussia all males were subject to call up for the army. Discipline was cruel. Training and drilling went on for hours. The sons of peasants and the sons of noblemen became hardened, vicious soldiers. The whole country became military minded and proud of its famous fighters.

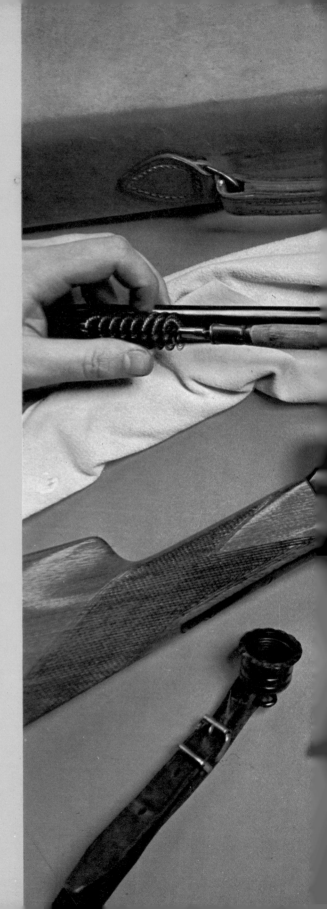

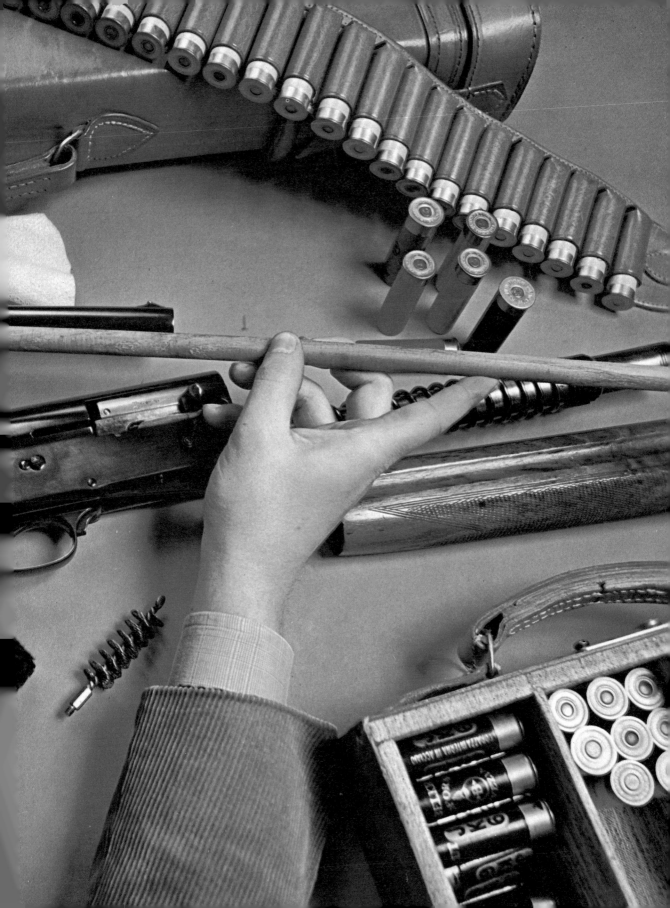

120

A world alone and apart

To the people of Europe, the lands of Russia seemed to be a world alone and apart. They knew very little about Russia. They imagined it to be a vast land to the east. This land was largely uninhabited by people. Wild animals roamed the dense forests, and polar bears and seals lived in the vast Siberian wasteland that was covered with ice and snow for three-quarters of the year.

It was difficult for people then, as now, to realize just how big Russia really is. In the west Russia begins at the eastern borders of Europe. Even today a train will take ten days to travel across Russia to the Pacific Ocean, its eastern border. From the Arctic Circle in the north, Russia stretches 6,500 kilometres (4,000 miles) south to the borders of India. For many centuries, adventurous merchants travelled to Russia to trade in precious furs and other goods. Apart from that, Russia and her people had little real contact with Europe until the 1700s, the eighteenth century.

Trimming the Russians' beards

Peter the Great ruled Russia as Tsar (the Russian title for king or emperor) from 1682 to 1725. Peter modernized the Russian nation, for he realized that the West had made great advances. His own vast country had not. Peter set out to reform Russia after a voyage to the West in 1697. That year marks a dividing line in the whole history of Russia. Before 1697, Russia was a nation looking in upon itself, eastern and barbaric in its ways. After 1697, Russia became more civilized, and contact with the West has never been totally lost.

Peter changed some part of almost everything in Russian life—styles of dress, social customs, laws, military and governmental systems, trade, science, art, and education.

One of the things that Peter did which shocked the Russians was to order men to trim their beards. Almost two centuries before, the Tsar, Ivan the Terrible, had said: "To shave the beard is a sin that the blood of all the martyrs cannot cleanse. Is it not

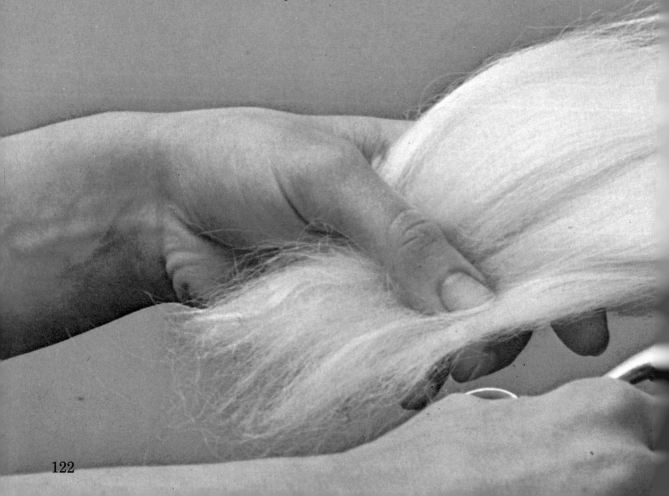

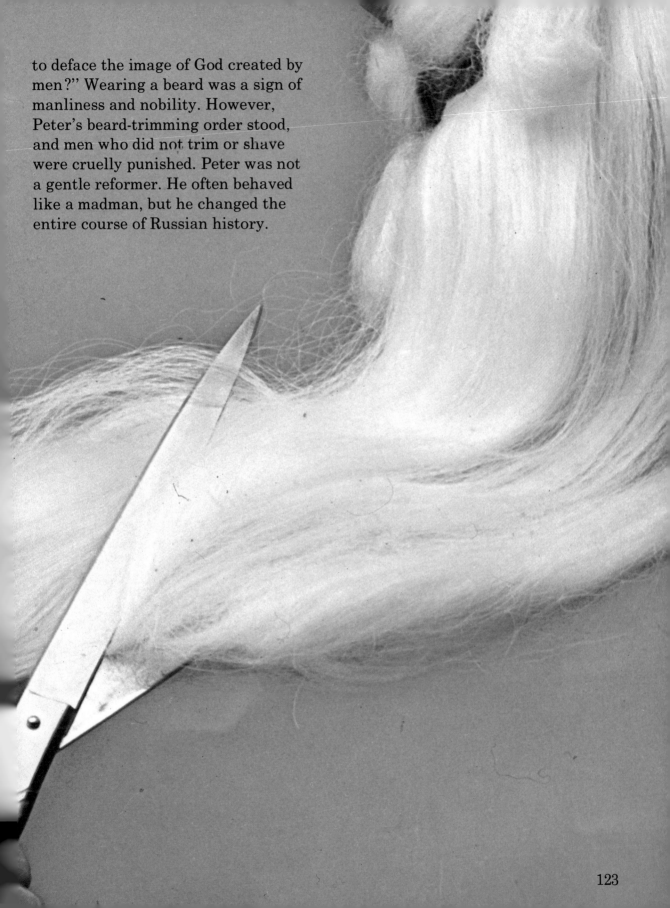

to deface the image of God created by men?" Wearing a beard was a sign of manliness and nobility. However, Peter's beard-trimming order stood, and men who did not trim or shave were cruelly punished. Peter was not a gentle reformer. He often behaved like a madman, but he changed the entire course of Russian history.

Drilling holes in water

The eighteenth century was a time when rulers, their advisers, and ministers of state began to realize that reforms and changes in their countries were needed. The population of Europe was growing, so more people had to be able to earn a living. Better ways of doing business and of engaging in trade made life easier and richer. So did more widespread education and learning in all areas. Wars created much poverty and misery, and made small and large countries poorer rather than rich and secure.

Many changes and reforms did little to improve the everyday life of people. Sometimes changes were useless, or the ways and means employed to make changes were useless. Imagine someone trying to drill a hole in the bottom of a small stream. If he wants to make a hole, he will have to dam the stream first, or the hole will just keep filling up with water. Some changes take a lot of effort and planning.

Some of the changes and reforms in the life of European peoples were undertaken in such a useless way.

Obedience and freedom

Most of the states and countries of Europe were
ruled by absolute monarchs in the eighteenth
century. However, these were a different kind of
absolute ruler. Rulers no longer had the same
kind of absolute power as had Louis XIV, France's
Sun King. In this century, rulers were
"enlightened". Enlighten means to "shed light on".
In other words, rulers saw their role as rulers in a
different light. So did their subjects, the people
they ruled.

Men now believed that countries were best
governed by a powerful ruler, but that the ruler
should keep the peoples' best interests in mind as
he or she went about the work.

Enlightened rulers tried to increase food

production and trade. They often tried to improve the life of peasant farmers. Fairer and more just laws were made. Horrible punishments for crimes were lessened. Education was encouraged. Rulers mostly let people follow the religion they chose.

People felt they had much more freedom, but rulers still demanded obedience. Where people had been kept firmly on a leash by their rulers before, now rulers seemed to take off the leashes. Rulers, however, were serving their own interests more than those of their subjects. Soon, people would demand real freedom. They would question why they should be obedient to a ruler at all. Enlightened monarchs tried to make changes to keep people happier, but most people preferred freedom to choose what they wanted.

War in Europe

Changes in the ways of governing people had made life better in the eighteenth century. However, between 1740 and 1763, most of Europe was a battleground. At the start, Catholic Austria fought Protestant Prussia over possession of Silesia. This tiny part of the Austrian empire was a rich linen-making centre. The conflicts which resulted involved not only Prussia and Austria, but France, Russia, Spain, Italy and Holland. Each country had something to gain from a war, and sometimes they fought as enemies and sometimes they joined forces to attack another enemy.

England, France, and Spain fought because they were trading rivals. They went to war on the high seas and in foreign lands where merchants had built trading centres.

By 1763 when peace treaties put an end, for the time being, to the rivalry among European powers, the people of Europe were exhausted. Army after army had trampled over their lands, eating their food, killing their animals, burning their homes, stealing and plundering. The fortunes and misfortunes of war destroyed the spirit of harmony and order. People were tired of being used and abused. A spirit of discord-and disorder spread throughout Europe. Enlightened rulers made life just as miserable for people as unenlightened rulers had.

Trāsla.B.Hiero.

Septimo autem anno sabbatum ... terre requieti domini. Agrum non seres: & vineā non putabis. Que spōte gignet humus non metes. & ... primitiarū ... cōlligere quasi vindemiā. Annus enī requietiōis terre est. Sed erunt vobis in cibū: tibi & seruo tuo: ancille & mercenario tuo: & aduene q peregrinatur apud te. Iumetis tuis & pecoribus omnia que nascentur prebebunt cibum. Numerabis quoq tibi septem hebdomadas annorū.i.septies septē. que simul faciunt quadraginta ani. & annumerabitis ... quadraginta noue. & clanges buccina mense septimo decima die mensis propitiationis tempore in vniuersa terra vestra. Sanctificabisq annum quinquagesimum. & vocabis remissione cūctis hitatoribus terre tue. Ipse est enim iubileus. Reuertetur hō ad possessione suā: & vnusquisq rediet ad familiā pristinā. qa iubileus est. & quinquagesimus annus. Nō seretis atq metetis spōte in agro nascētia. & primitias vindemie nō colligetis ob sctificatione iubilei: sed stati ablata comedetis.

Interp.chal.

Anno aūt septimo requies remissionis erit terre: remissio erit corā dño:agrū tuū nō seres:& vineā tuā nō putabis. ... quae spōte nascitur terre nō metes: & vuas quae tibi reliquisti nō vindemiabis: annus eni remissionis terre. Eritq remissio terre vobis in cibū tibi & seruo tuo: & ancille tue: & mercenario tuo: & inquilino tuo qui habitat tecū: iumetis quoq tuis & bestie q sunt in terra tua erit omnia fructus eius in cibū. Numerabis tibi septē hebdomadas annorū: septē annos: septies. tibi erunt ... quadraginta & nouem anni. Et transire facies buccina clangoris mense septimo: decima mensis: in die expiationis: transire facies buccina in vniuersa terra vestra. Et sanctificabitis annū quinquagesimū: & vocabitis libertatem in terra cunctis habitatoribus eius. Iubileus erit vobis: & reuertetur vnusquisq ad possessionem suam: & vnusquisq reuertetur ad familiā suam. Iubileus est: annus quinquagesimus erit vobis. Non seminabitis neq metetis eq sponte nascitur in terra:neq putabitis reliquia eius. Quia iubileus est: sanctus erit vobis: de agro comedetis fructus eius.

ꝓ iij

The enlightenment

...or the Age of Reason

At the end of the seventeenth and beginning of the eighteenth centuries, educated men wanted to shed light on (or enlighten) all kinds of knowledge. They believed that people could and should think clearly (and reasonably) for themselves. People should not just believe what they were told by other people. If men and women thought about all the things that happened in the world, clearly and reasonably, then all mankind could live together on earth more peacefully. Thinking for oneself and trying to understand things clearly were the important ideas in the Age of Reason, or the Enlightenment.

A French philosopher, René Descartes, was one of the great thinkers of the age. He wrote a famous phrase: "I think, therefore I am." Descartes believed that the thoughts a man thinks are what makes that man what and who he is. His idea explains how men thought in the Age of Reason. They thought: "If any man thinks clearly and reasonably, then he *is* a clear-thinking, reasonable man. And reasonable men are not deliberately cruel. They do not engage in conflict. They try to make life better for themselves and for mankind."

Clear thinking can be used in all areas of life. Look at the different size coloured shapes. If you think about them clearly, you will see that they fit together, like a jigsaw puzzle, to make a square. Men in the Age of Reason believed that the problems of life could be solved like the puzzle, if men thought clearly and reasonably.

Experience and reason

If you have waited for a bus at a bus stop, you will know that life is better if people form an orderly line and wait their turn. If everyone rushes towards the bus when it arrives, and pushes everyone else out of the way, life can be very difficult and unpleasant. So there is a very good reason for forming a queue, and that is why people do it.

An English philosopher called John Locke thought that when a man is born, his mind is like a blank piece of paper just waiting to be written on. And the "writing" that goes onto the empty page is the person's experience, which means the things which happen to him. Part of the "writing" is the type of conditions (or environment) the person lives in. Some of it is what he is taught (education). All these things add up to a full mind, like a crowded page. They make the man what he is. Today we know that our living conditions (or environment) are very important. They help make us the kind of people we are. But this was a new idea in the seventeenth and eighteenth centuries.

The men of the Age of Reason hoped that the more people learned about themselves, the more reasonably they would behave. This would make life better for everyone.

The brain
and the heart

The greatest thinker of the Age of Reason was the French writer Voltaire. His life spanned most of the eighteenth century, which is sometimes called the Age of Voltaire. He lived in England for three years, and he was astounded by these free, lively, educated, reasonable men. At the time, England was the freest country of Europe. Voltaire was practical, witty, and brilliant. He can be thought of as the "brain" of the Age of Reason.

Voltaire firmly believed that man should look with clear eyes about himself, see the evils that exist, and try to cure them with reason. He made John Locke's ideas popular in Europe. All his life, Voltaire battled for reason, for human freedom, for a more fair, more just, and more dignified life for man.

Jean Jacques Rousseau was another great French thinker of the Age. He could be called its "heart". Rousseau believed that men were naturally good. He thought that too much learning and reason made men unhappy. Rousseau believed that men were happy when they saw less and knew less of evil—when they acted naturally, emotionally, then they could live together in a state of order and harmony. In a book called *Candide*, Voltaire made cruel fun of a naturally good man who believed he could find "all for the best in this best of all possible worlds".

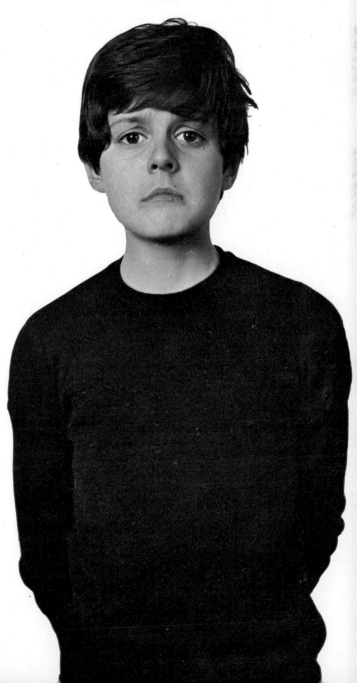

The power of printing

The ideas of the Enlightenment and the Age of Reason spread quickly and became popular. Noblemen, scholars, the growing educated middle classes, some craftsmen and a few country people were all reading. They found the new ideas exciting and the printing of books expanded to meet the new demand.

In many countries, books and pamphlets were censored. This means they could only be published and sold if rulers, the government, or the Church approved of them. The new ideas frightened those in power—they recognized that words in print had power to make people want to change their lives.

Many small private printing presses were set up to publish the new ideas. Men worked in dark rooms, setting up letters in type for printing or copying words out by hand. These secretly printed or copied works were passed from hand to hand. Censorship helped spread the ideas, because people are always curious about forbidden things.

Paris, especially, became a hotbed of excitement over the ideas of reason and freedom for men. This led to the French Revolution in 1789. The ideas about freedom and the rights of men caught the imagination of a people who were harshly ruled by an absolute monarch.

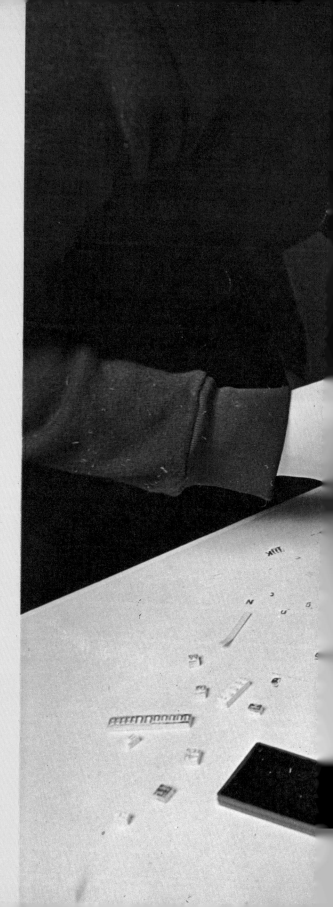

Freedom takes wing

Like a butterfly emerging from its cocoon, freedom began to take wing in the Age of Reason. At first, these ideas only fluttered faintly like a newly emerged butterfly. With the impact of the French Revolution, men everywhere in the western world began to take notice of the new ideas. They began to want liberty and equality.

Rulers throughout Europe were terrified. For centuries, their right to rule had been unchallenged. Now the common people wanted an end to special privileges for noblemen, for the churches, and for kings. Common men demanded the right to have a say in the laws that were passed. They demanded a say in the way they were ruled. They wanted a better life for themselves and for their children. Above all, they demanded freedom of thought and freedom to speak and write as they wished. Now common men were convinced that governments or kings should rule for the benefit of their people, not for themselves.

Jean Jacques Rousseau had put the problem of freedom clearly before the people. He wrote: Man is born free but is everywhere in chains. Men determined to unchain themselves. The age of calm and reason inspired rioting, bloodshed, and revolution. The purpose of the conflicts was different from previous conflicts. Men were fighting for themselves and for their future.

Rich discoveries

Sweet reward

If a bee landed by mistake on a large lollipop, it would find a
new source of rich sweetness. When the European nations began
searching for a quicker and easier route to the East, they
discovered, by mistake, other large continents. America,
Africa, and parts of Asia were a surprisingly sweet and rich
discovery to these exploring Europeans.

At first, the Portuguese, the Spanish, the French, the English, and the Dutch established small seaports where they landed. From these settlements, they could gather and ship back to Europe any native goods or riches worth trading. As trade expanded, the settlements expanded. In many places, permanent colonies were established. A colony is a settlement of people who leave their native land to live in another land. The members of the colony remain loyal to their mother land. The colony is governed by or subject to the mother country. Most of the powerful European countries established permanent colonies in America or Africa or Asia.

Native riches

The native, or local, goods found in the Americas made merchants, kings, and countries rich. Portugal and Spain had discovered the gold and silver in Central America, and made their countries rich for some years.

As time passed, more explorers, followed by adventurous merchants, sailed to the American continent. More goods were discovered which fetched huge prices back home in the lively European markets.

Coffee and cocoa beans fetched high prices once it was discovered that they could be made into delicious liquids. Rich Europeans paid high prices for these fashionable products. Great fortunes were made by merchants who would brave the long sea journeys and the squalid living conditions in the colonies. Tobacco, maize, potatoes, sugar cane, and the pelts of animals like beaver and seal became prized in Europe.

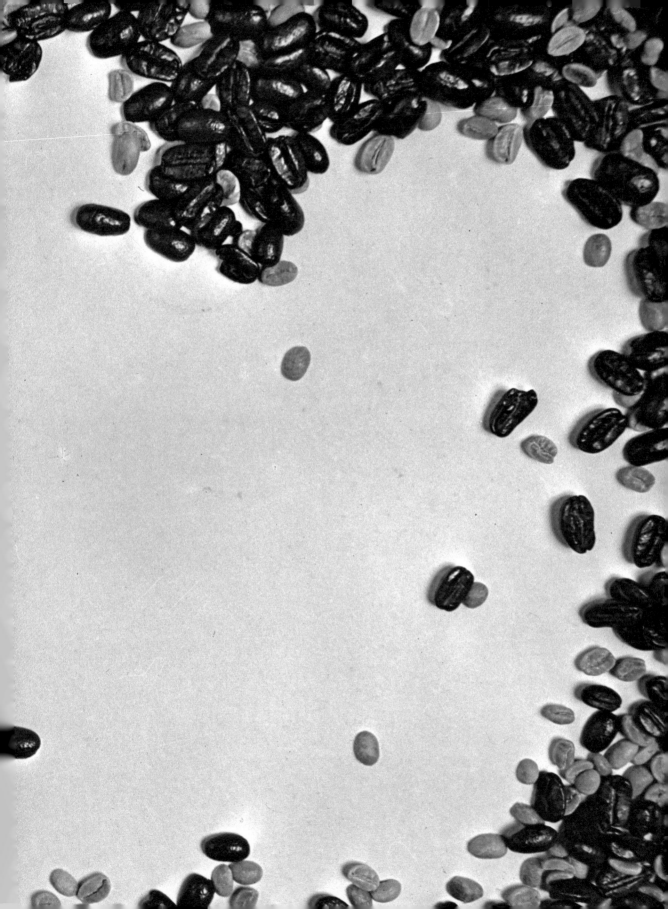

Carving up the Americas

No one needs a carving knife to cut a pudding. It can easily be spooned out in small portions, one at a time. At first the European nations took small portions of the Americas for themselves. They planted their flags in small areas and trod cautiously on the foreign lands. Then they began slicing out large portions, just as if they were using a carving knife. The natives were astounded and provided little resistance, both in Central and in North America.

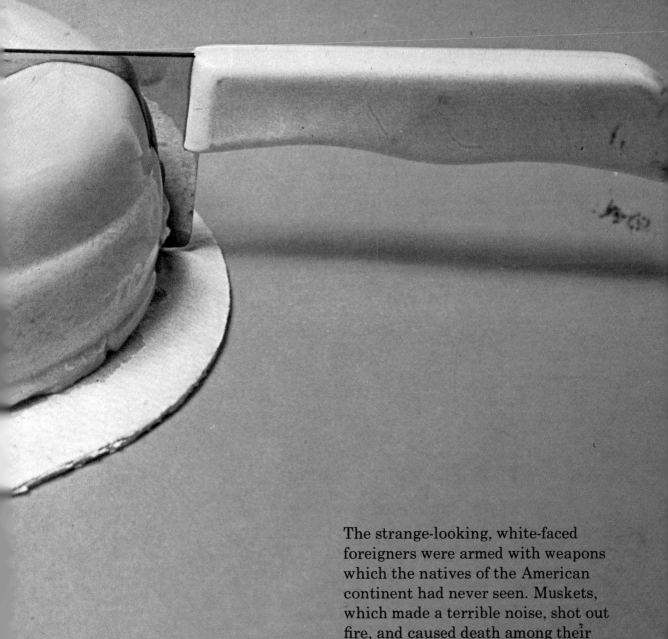

The strange-looking, white-faced foreigners were armed with weapons which the natives of the American continent had never seen. Muskets, which made a terrible noise, shot out fire, and caused death among their people, must have seemed like magic from the gods. The Europeans killed hundreds of natives in their attempts to grab goods and gold and silver to take back home. Explorers, and later merchants, were ruthless in America.

Men from Mars

The native peoples of the West Indies off the coast of America seemed very uncivilized to Christopher Columbus and other Spaniards who came to the New World. Inland, however, things were different. The Mayas, Incas, and Aztecs who lived there were organized and certainly not savages. They built aqueducts, roads, huge temples, and other buildings. They made beautiful jewellery of gold and of silver.

In 1519, a Spaniard, Hernando Cortés began his conquest of the mainland of Central America all the way to Mexico. To the Maya Indians, Cortés and his men must have seemed as strange as green creatures from another planet would seem to soldiers defending their country today. The Mayas were hostile to the Spanish at first, and Cortés' men shot cannons at them. The Indians had never seen horses, so Cortés made his horses gallop at full speed while their riders shouted and waved weapons in the air. The Mayas were struck with awe. They remembered an old prophecy which said gods in the shape of men with thunderbolts would conquer them and overthrow their king.

Within two years, Cortés and his men had conquered all of Mexico and had reduced its magnificent cities and native civilization to ruins.

Transporting home

After the conquest of Mexico, Spaniards, Portuguese, Frenchmen, Dutchmen, and Englishmen struggled for possession of lands in the Americas. The English were the most successful in establishing permanent colonies.

The Spaniards and most other Europeans were not permanent colonists in the way the English were. The Spanish, French, and Dutch came to the New World to exploit its riches. A few stayed, but most wanted to make a quick fortune and return home.

The English too wanted to make their fortunes from the New World. Many also intended to settle and stay there for the rest of their lives. Many Englishmen went to America to build a new life for themselves. They began to build colonies because they were escaping from religious persecution at home. Their independent ideas about God and worship made them seek a new land in which to worship in peace. When Englishmen went to America, they took their worldly goods with them. They transported as much of their English homes and homelife with them as they could.

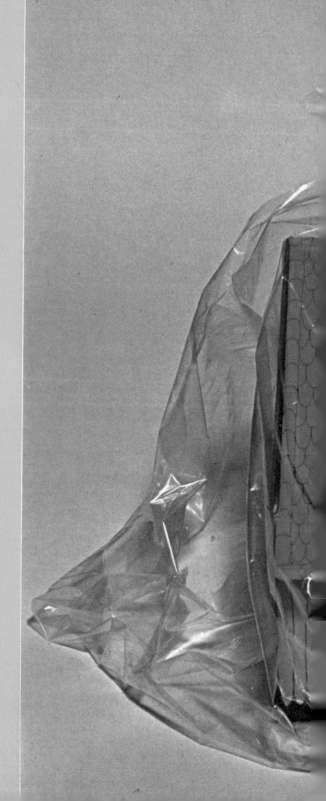

Flocking to America

Before long, the English were migrating to America like huge flocks of birds. As the original English colonists became able to make a new and comfortable life for themselves, the news reached England and spread. There was plenty of land to be had for free in the New World. There was a freedom of spirit which men in Europe had still not achieved.

The English and other Europeans were fascinated by the stories about America—its Red Indians, its wide open wild lands, its wildlife, its riches. In America all that counted was how hard a man worked. It didn't matter there whether a man had been born into a noble family or whether he was the son of a poor peasant farmer. In America, a man could be free, he could make himself rich, he could be respected for the work he did. The ideas about the freedom of man and the rights of man which were catching the imaginations of Europeans in the Age of Reason were being put into practice in America.

The French had gained a few footholds in North America, but they were outnumbered by the English. They fought a series of small wars, but slowly the English won and forced the few Frenchmen farther north into the wilds of Canada.

The Stars and Stripes

The Age of Reason turned into an age of revolutions. We know that France had a major revolution when the common people demanded freedom from an absolute monarch. Far away, in the New World, revolution came earlier. The thirteen original English colonies declared their independence from England on 4 July, 1776. The American colonists wanted freedom, too. In their Declaration of Independence they said that "all men are created equal" and that God had given men the right to "life, liberty and the pursuit of happiness".

Many causes led to the American Revolution. The colonies were a long way distant from their mother country. They had different religious views. Everyday life was very different. The colonies had no representative in the English parliament to present their views. England taxed the colonies on goods imported from overseas and taxed them to pay for English soldiers kept in the colonies. In 1775 the first shots were fired and war went on until 1781. The independence of America from England was officially proclaimed by the Treaty of Paris in 1783. From then on the "Stars and Stripes" (the popular nickname for the American flag) flew proudly over the newly free land.

Daring young men

All of Europe was shocked and
stunned by the American Revolution.
Here was a handful of small colonies
which had been settled for less than
one hundred and fifty years
challenging one of the most powerful
countries of Europe. The motley crew
of ill-equipped, sometimes starving
farmer-settlers had begun a war with
England and had won. Europe
marvelled at the daring of the young
colonies in the same way that we
marvel at the feats of trapeze artistes
in a circus.

Every friend of freedom in the Old
World felt excitement at the birth of
the new American nation. What the
American colonists had gained by
revolution, Europeans felt might be
gained at home by similar daring. The
birth of new ideas of freedom and
liberty in the Age of Reason now
seemed to go hand in hand with
revolution.

Once the spirit of freedom had
been aroused, it spread from America
to France. From the days of the
French Revolution to our own times,
man's quest for liberty goes on.
Both the American and, thirteen years
later, the French Revolution changed
the whole of man's history in the
western world.

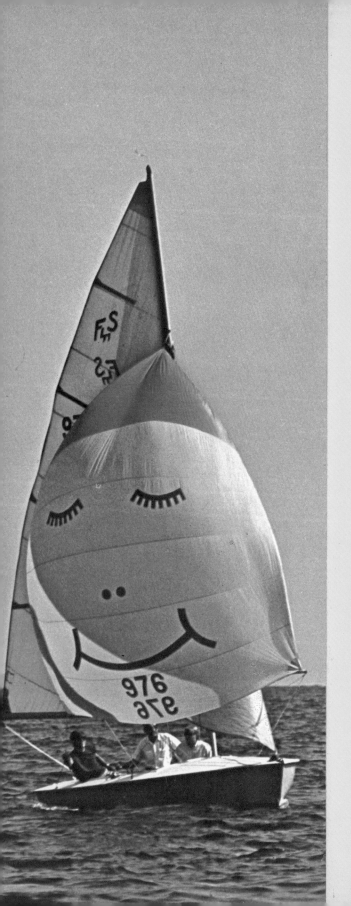

Happier times... new explorations

The American colonies gained their independence from England. The peoples of Europe gained more freedom for themselves. Kings and the churches which had once been so powerful lost much of their power over men's lives. The world was no longer sharply divided between noblemen and commoners. Life was more varied. A vast middle class of people was becoming richer and more powerful. Men's lives were happier and they had more freedom.

New ideas about the world and about man's place in it excited men's minds and led them to even more exciting discoveries. Education and knowledge were more widespread.

While life had changed greatly from the fifteenth to the eighteenth centuries, men still had only the smallest knowledge about the planet on which they lived. Other ships, quite different from the happy sailing boat in the picture, were still to cross the great oceans and discover lands as yet unknown to Europeans. Explorers would search the far corners of the earth in the nineteenth century, acquiring new knowledge about man's home—the earth.

Index